Baking & Pastry

Basic Techniques

Lesley Chesterman
Bertrand Bazin

MACMILLAN CANADA
TORONTO

First published in English in Canada in 2000 by
Macmillan Canada, an imprint of CDG Books Canada

Canadian Cataloguing in Publication Data

Chesterman, Lesley, 1967 —
Basic cooking techniques : bakery and pastry

Translation of: Pâtisserie et boulangerie.
Includes index.
ISBN 0-7715-7711-7

1. Baking. 2. Pastry I. Bazin, Bertrand, 1967 — II. Title.

TX763.C4313 2000 641.8'15 C00-932271-X

This book is available at special discounts for bulk purchases by your group or organization for sales promotions, premiums, fundraising and seminars. For details, contact: CDG Books Canada Inc., 99 Yorkville Avenue, Suite 400, Toronto, ON, M5R 3K5.

1 2 3 4 5 TOTAL 04 03 02 01 00

Design and typesetting:	Cyclone Design Communications
Photography:	François Croteau
Project manager:	Gisèle LaRocque
Linguistic revision:	Mark Daly and Katrin Sermat
Proofreading:	Jane Jackel
Indexing:	Diane Baril

Macmillan Canada
An imprint of CDG Books Canada Inc.
Toronto

Printed in Canada

CONTENTS

Introduction	5
Getting Started	6
Equipment	8
Basic Techniques	10
Doughs	13
Basic Cakes	21
Creams, Fillings and Sauces	31
Pies and Tarts	47
Classic Cakes	63
Petits Fours	87
Yeast Breads	97
Quick Breads	113
Index	126

Introduction

Introduction

Practice makes perfect and nowhere is this maxim more appropriate than in the world of pastry and baking. Many excellent home cooks confess that baking is their downfall. Unlike regular cooking, pastry crusts and fruit tarts aren't things you make everyday. It would therefore be unrealistic to expect perfection your first time around — or even your second. In point of fact, it's not as difficult as it appears. But like learning to play the piano, it does take plenty of practice and patience.

It isn't easy to explain pastry making in words because so much of it is about feeling: the smoothness of a mound of dough that is neither too dry nor too sticky ... the unctuousness of a custard cream coating the back of a wooden spoon ... the bounce of a freshly baked sponge cake as it emerges from the oven ... the elasticity of bread dough after ten minutes of intense kneading. In an effort to explain these feelings, we've added many technique pictures to help illustrate the look of the product and the process involved in making it.

You may have successfully mastered some of these recipes in the past. Others may appear long and difficult — definitely not for the beginner. Our advice is to go slowly. Don't try the croissant recipe until you've had some success making puff pastry and bread.

You may wonder why we've even bothered including a croissant recipe when croissants are available at your local bakery. My answer is, just for the thrill of it. As you're about to discover, there's nothing more satisfying than savouring a croissant or Danish made lovingly from scratch.

Many people find that baking is a relaxing pastime. This may turn out to be your experience as well. Rest assured that once you've mastered a few techniques, steady progress is inevitable. Pretty soon you won't think twice about including one or more of these creations at your get-together.

The first part of the book focuses on basic pastry recipes. The second puts the basic recipes together to form cakes and tarts. The last part is devoted to yeast and quick breads. Advanced bakers may eventually try using these recipes to create their own original cakes and tarts.

Before you crack an egg or sift a cup of flour, here are three helpful hints: 1) read through the first few pages outlining the ingredients and equipment used in the book, 2) try to use the freshest, best quality ingredients you can find, and 3) weigh out all the listed ingredients before starting a recipe to be sure you have everything on hand.

One last thought. Pastry can be so much more than a sugary close to a meal. With a few choice recipes in your repertoire, you can enliven a weekend brunch, spruce up an afternoon tea, cap a friend's birthday party — even give a thrill to an insomniac on his or her nocturnal trip to the refrigerator.

Now, how's that for incentive?

Getting Started

Getting Started

Always read through a recipe to make sure you have the necessary ingredients on hand before starting. If you aren't an experienced baker, you should read about the ingredients used in the book to know exactly what to purchase. Even the experienced baker should have a look at this list to be sure the ingredients we use are the same ones he or she uses.

Butter: All recipes in the book call for unsalted butter. Unsalted butter is more perishable than salted and should be kept refrigerated no more than a week and frozen if kept for longer periods of time. It also absorbs surrounding odours easily, so be sure to keep onions and garlic far away. It's important to follow instructions regarding butter temperature. For recipes that call for creamed butter (room temperature butter), it is best to remove the butter from the refrigerator the night before it is needed.

Chocolate: Semisweet and bittersweet chocolate are a pastry chef's first choice for making chocolate desserts. When purchasing, look for high quality dark, milk or white chocolate with a cocoa butter content of at least 22%. The taste of your dessert is based on the amount of cocoa liquor and sugar in the chocolate. Its texture (especially for mousses or ganache) is based on the cocoa butter content. Favoured brands include Valrhona, Barry-Callebaut, DGF, Lindt, Suchard and Ghirardelli. Baker's is also an acceptable brand.

Cocoa powder: Look for dark cocoa with a cocoa butter content of at least 22%. Valrhona, Cacao-Barry and Van Houten make excellent cocoa powder. The problem with many other cocoa powders is that their colour is pale and the flavour too weak to achieve a rich chocolate taste and look. Cocoa powders mixed with sugar, such as instant cocoa mix, should not be substituted for cocoa powder in these recipes.

Eggs: All recipes in this book use large calibre eggs, with a yolk weighing 20 g and the white 30 g. It is important to use the freshest eggs for custard-based preparations. Cake batters actually whip up better with eggs that are about a week old. This is especially true for meringues. Eggs can be separated either cold or at room temperature. We have no preference.

Flour: The pastry section of this book uses mainly all-purpose flour, a cross between bread and pastry flours. Bread flour, which is higher in gluten, is the flour needed for the heavier, elastic bread dough made with yeast. An elastic dough better traps the gas bubbles formed by the yeast, which causes the dough to rise. Egg-based batters sometimes call for lighter pastry and cake flours which are low in gluten. If possible, always buy unbleached white flour. All flour should be stored in an airtight container and can be kept for up to six months at room temperature. Whole wheat and many specialty flours can turn rancid and should be kept either refrigerated or frozen. In warmer months, keep flours mould-and bug-free by storing them in the refrigerator or freezer.

Gelatin: Gelatin can be purchased in two forms: powdered gelatin or sheet gelatin. Powdered gelatin must be "bloomed," that is softened in cold water for at least 1 minute — count a 1/4 cup (50 mL) of water for every 2 teaspoons (7 g) of gelatin. Sheet gelatin must be softened in plenty of cold water for about 5 minutes. Remove from the water and squeeze out the excess liquid before using. Softened gelatin, in either form, should be stirred into a hot liquid in order to dissolve properly.

Marzipan: Commercially available in many supermarkets, gourmet shops or cake-decorating stores in well-sealed packages or cans as either almond paste or marzipan. It can be coloured and formed into shapes or rolled like dough into a sheet to cover a cake (like the fraisier on page 75). Cake batters made with marzipan have a wonderful almond flavour and moist texture. Marzipan should not be refrigerated or frozen for long periods of time since it has a high sugar content and will "weep" and melt in such a humid environment. Keep marzipan wrapped in plastic at all times or it will become crusty or dry to a rock-hard consistency. Treat marzipan with care. Be sure it is handled with immaculately clean hands.

Milk and cream: Heavy cream (fat content between 30% and 35%, also known as whipping cream) is the only one called for in this book. Milk can be either whole milk, 2%, skim or UHT (ultra high temperature). Be sure all dairy products are as fresh as possible and kept well chilled until ready to use.

Nuts: Try to buy the freshest nuts possible and always store them in the freezer. Many fruit stores and gourmet shops carry higher quality nuts than your corner store or supermarket. Some nuts can be substituted for others. If a recipe calls for pecans, walnuts can be used in their place — and vice versa.

Praline paste: Praline is made with caramelized nuts, either almonds or hazelnuts or a combination of both, ground to a fine, smooth paste. Think of it as a high-end peanut butter. It can be difficult to find but look for it in gourmet shops, cake-decorating stores, or ask the owner of your local pastry shop to sell you a cup.

Salt: Salt is essential for the flavour, colour and texture of pastry and baked products. It is best to use a fine-grained refined salt (table salt) for these recipes.

Sugar: Granulated sugar is the one used most frequently in this book. Icing sugar (also called powdered or confectioner's sugar) should always be sifted before use. All sugars should be kept clean (keep out the flour!) and in individual well-sealed containers, especially brown sugar.

Vegetable oil spray: Oil sprays are a good alternative to buttering a pan for especially sticky or delicate batters such as madeleines. Always use these sprays sparingly and be sure to use an unflavoured product.

Vegetable shortening: Solid white vegetable shortening is used to make flaky pie crusts. Though many bakers use it in place of butter to cut costs, don't forget that though you are saving money, you will be cutting down considerably on flavour.

Yeast: All recipes in this book call for dry yeast. It is good to know that one 8 g package of yeast equals 2 1/4 teaspoons. Fresh or cake yeast can be substituted if you double the amount, by weight, called for in a recipe using dry yeast — e.g.: 12 g of dry yeast can be replaced by 25 g of fresh yeast. Dissolve fresh yeast in the liquid in your recipe, warm or cold. Only then can it come into contact with salt, otherwise the salt will kill the yeast. Always activate the yeast (proofing) in a warm liquid with a pinch of sugar to be sure it is alive before continuing with a recipe.

Equipment

Equipment

Baking sheets, cake pans, bread moulds: Standard baking sheets 17- by 11-inch (42 by 28 cm), 9- by 1 3/4-inch (23 by 5 cm) or 8- by 1 3/4-inch (20 by 5 cm) cake pans, and 8- by 4 inch (20 by 10 cm) loaf pans are what is called for in the book. If possible, look for pans with a nonstick surface.

Pastry rings and springform pans: A pastry ring is a bottomless, stainless steel ring which is placed on a parchment-lined baking sheet. The ring needed for the recipes in this book is 8- by 2 1/2-inch (20 by 6 cm). If you can't find a pastry ring at a cake-decorating shop or kitchen supply store, you can use a spring form pan. The only disadvantage of a spring form pan is that the sides are sloped and your cake will not be perfectly symmetrical.

French tart moulds and pie plates: A metal French tart mould has a fluted edge and a removable bottom. The one needed for these recipes is 9 in. (23 cm) wide and 1 in. (2.5 cm) high. These moulds rust easily so be sure to dry them thoroughly after washing. For a variation on shape, look for rectangular, square and individual French tart moulds.

Measuring cups, measuring spoons or scales: You will need a set of measuring cups and spoons for the recipes in this book. If you are using the metric measures, an accurate scale and metric measuring cup will be needed.

Pastry brushes: Pastry brushes can be purchased at cake-decorating shops or kitchen specialty stores. They are used mainly to brush apricot glaze onto a tart and soak syrup into a cake or dust off the flour from a sheet of dough. Make sure to keep them clean. Be careful of any loose bristles.

Rolling pin: Any rolling pin you are comfortable with is fine. You may prefer a large heavy rolling pin for tough dough like puff pastry.

Strainers and sifters: You will need a fine mesh strainer for sifting dry ingredients and straining delicate creams and sauces. A hand-held flour sifter is not recommended.

Electric mixer: Hand-held or upright, an electric mixer is an essential tool in pastry making. Many bread and cookie recipes can be made without it, but sponge cakes and emulsified creams are practically impossible to make without an electric mixer. Upright, heavy duty mixers can also be used to knead bread dough.

Ruler or tape measure: For measuring dough and pan sizes.

Spatulas and offset spatulas: Spatulas are the most important tool for spreading and icing. Offset spatulas are used for spreading cake batter or cookies that are already in a baking pan. Straight spatulas are used for icing cakes. Look for triangle spatulas, which are ideal for smoothing the sides of a cake, in your hardware store.

Whisks: It's good to have a few different size whisks in your kitchen. Be sure to purchase whisks with thin wires.

Wooden spoons: Be sure all wooden spoons are clean, odourless and splinter-free.

Rubber spatulas and plastic scrapers: A rubber spatula is the best tool for folding airy mixtures together and scraping a bowl clean. A hand-held plastic scraper works the same way as a rubber spatula and is especially useful for heavy dough and batters.

Zester: Used to grate lemon or orange peel. For the finest grated zest, look for a microplane grater.

Pastry bags and tips: Pastry bags are essential for piping cookies, cakes and creams in many shapes and sizes. Pastry bags are inexpensive so it is a good idea to buy a few sizes. A large bag, 16 in. (40 cm), is good for piping cookies and choux pastry. A small bag, 8 in. (20 cm), is good for piping icing onto a cake. A mid-sized bag, 12 in. (30 cm), is practical as well. Look for soft, pliable bags made of either cloth or thin plastic. Disposable bags are also available. Round and fluted tips inserted into the base of the bag determine the shape that will be piped.

Marble slab: Useful as a cold surface for rolling pastry. If possible, look for one small enough to fit in your refrigerator.

Candy thermometer: Used to measure the temperature of boiled sugar syrups, they are vailable in many supermarkets and gourmet stores. Very fragile, never place a hot candy thermometer in cold water.

Parchment paper, Silpat® sheets: Parchment paper is a waterproof, heatproof paper that is ideal for nonstick cooking and baking. It can be purchased in rolls and individual sheets. Reusable and washable thick rubber Silpat® mats are another nonstick baking option. They are imported from France and therefore expensive, but if well-maintained, can be used for years. Look for them in cake-decorating stores.

Blowtorch: Used to facilitate unmoulding, by gently heating the sides of a pastry ring. Not essential but handy.

Basic Techniques

Basic Techniques

Filling a pastry bag: Turn down the pastry bag to make a cuff. This will keep the top of the bag clean. Place your pastry tip inside the bag. If your pastry bag is new, you may have to trim the opening. Be careful: if you trim off too much your tip will fall through the bottom and your bag will be ruined.

Piping with a pastry bag: Never fill your pastry bag completely — three-quarters full is fine. Push your filling to the base of the bag near the tip. Gather the top of the pastry bag and twist shut. With one hand, apply pressure on the top of the bag to gently squeeze out the filling. Place the fingers of your other hand around the base of the tip to guide you. Try to pipe quite closely to the work surface, either straight up and down or on a slant. To avoid air pockets, it is best to empty the pastry bag completely before refilling.

Chopping chocolate and making chocolate shavings: Large pieces of chocolate should be chopped with a large sharp knife on a cutting board. Placing your slab of chocolate in the microwave for about ten seconds will soften it slightly, making it easier to cut. You will need a block of chocolate to make chocolate shavings. Run a vegetable peeler along a flat edge of the chocolate. If the chocolate flakes instead of curling, run your hand along the surface to warm it up.

Melting chocolate on a bain-marie: Always chop chocolate into small pieces to facilitate melting. Chocolate will burn over a direct heat source, therefore it must be melted over a pot of simmering (not boiling) water. You can also use a microwave. Melt the chocolate on high heat for thirty seconds, stir, and continue for no more than thirty seconds at a time on medium heat. Watch it carefully and stir often or the intense heat will scorch the chocolate. Chocolate should never be melted above 120°F (49°C), which should feel only a little warmer than body temperature.

Using a vanilla bean: Vanilla beans should be sliced open and the seeds should be scraped out with the back of a knife. The beans and the cut pod should be placed in a liquid to infuse the flavour. Be sure to remove the pod and strain the infused liquid before proceeding with the recipe.

Flouring a work surface: Always throw flour, instead of sprinkling, onto your work surface to ensure a thin even layer. Keep the flour on your work surface to a minimum.

Folding ingredients together: Folding is a technique used to gently combine light and airy ingredients together without deflating the air in the mixture. To successfully fold ingredients, use a rubber spatula and lift the batter from the bottom of the bowl and fold over the top of the mixture, while turning your bowl with the other hand. Ingredients of compatible textures are easiest to combine.

How to measure dry and wet ingredients: Always measure dry ingredients by using the dip and scoop method: dip your measuring cup into the powder (flour, sugar, etc.) and scoop up the powder, then level off the powder with a knife or your finger. Liquid ingredients should always be measured in a clean, accurate measuring cup. For metric measures, dry ingredients are measured in grams and liquid ingredients are measured in millilitres.

Sifting ingredients: Dry ingredients should always be sifted, especially when there is a combination of many. We prefer to sift onto a parchment paper rather than a bowl. When a recipe says to sift together the dry ingredients, this does not include the sugar.

Separating eggs: Eggs must be separated using their shells. Crack the egg on a sharp edge over a bowl, separate the shell in half, keeping the yolk in one of the shell halves and letting the white fall into the bowl. Transfer the yolk into the other half, letting the excess white drip off the side. Repeat this process three or four times until the yolk and white are separated. If a small amount of yolk falls into the white, use the side of an empty eggshell to scoop it out. Be careful: if too much yolk falls into the whites, you will not be able to whisk them to a froth.

Peeling and coring fruit: It is best to use a fixed blade vegetable peeler to peel and core fruit since it will remove the least amount of flesh. Always start by cutting off the top and bottom of the fruit with the end of the peeler. Then, using the top of your peeler, dig out the top and bottom of the core. Peel the fruit using an up and down motion. Scoop out the remaining core with a melon baller.

Doughs
Doughs

Shortcrust Pastry
Sweet Shortcrust Pastry
Puff Pastry
Egg Wash
Choux Pastry

Pâte brisée, also known as shortcrust pastry in French means, "broken dough," which refers to the crumbly texture of the final product.

Shortcrust Pastry ~ Pâte Brisée

INGREDIENTS

2 2/3 cups all-purpose flour **400 g**
1 tablespoon sugar **12 g**
1/2 teaspoon salt **3 g**
1/2 cup unsalted butter, cold **125 g**
1/2 cup vegetable shortening **125 g**
1/2 cup ice water **125 mL**

METHOD

1. Sift the dry ingredients together in a bowl or on a clean tabletop.
2. With a knife or metal dough cutter, cut the fats into the dry ingredients. Break the butter and shortening down into smaller pea-sized pieces with your hands.
3. Make a well, and pour water into the centre.
4. Gradually incorporate the dry ingredients with the water.
5. Mix gently until just combined. Do not overwork the dough or it will be tough.
6. Wrap in plastic and refrigerate at least 1 hour before rolling.

Makes enough dough for a double 9-inch (23 cm) crust covered pie or two 9-inch (23 cm) single crust tart shells

Storage: Wrap well.
Refrigerator: 2 days.
Freezer: Up to 6 weeks.

This sweet dough is perfect for cookie-like crusts used for fruit tarts, lemon tarts, chocolate tarts and almond tarts. To facilitate the rolling process, this recipe makes more dough than you will need to fill a tart shell.

Sweet Shortcrust Pastry ~ PÂTE SUCRÉE

INGREDIENTS

3/4 cup unsalted butter, room temperature **170 g**

2/3 cup icing sugar **75 g**

Pinch salt

2 egg yolks **2**

2 tablespoons ice water **30 mL**

1 2/3 cups all-purpose flour, sifted **250 g**

METHOD

1. Beat the butter until smooth and creamy.
2. Blend in the icing sugar and salt.
3. Add the egg yolks one by one, followed by the water.
4. Stir in the flour. Turn the dough onto a lightly floured counter and crush with the base of your palm to combine the dough without overworking it (see photos).
5. Shape the dough into a flat round disk, wrap in plastic and refrigerate at least 2 hours before rolling.

Makes enough dough for an 8-, 9- or 10-inch (20 to 26 cm) tart shell

Storage: Wrap well
Refrigerator: 2 days.
Freezer: Up to 6 weeks.

Puff Pastry

Puff pastry is used to make pastries such as mille-feuilles, cheese straws and flaky tarts. It is quite difficult to succeed on your first try. The key to making good puff pastry is to always let the dough rest between turns and to make sure the butter remains cold. In dry weather, a few extra tablespoons of water may be needed for the base dough, which should be firm and smooth without being sticky or dry.

Puff Pastry ~ Pâte feuilletée

INGREDIENTS

3 3/4 cups all-purpose flour **562 g**
1 tablespoon salt **20 g**
1 1/4 cups ice water **310 mL**
3 tablespoons melted butter **45 mL**
2 cups unsalted butter, cold **454 g**

METHOD

1 Sift the flour onto the work surface.

2 Whisk together the water and the salt.

3 Make a well in the flour, pour in the salted water along with the melted butter and incorporate the flour into the liquid.

4 "Strangle the dough" (see picture) by squeezing it in sections; knead lightly into a smooth ball, cut an X in the top, wrap and refrigerate 1 hour.

5 Meanwhile, place the cold butter between 2 pieces of parchment paper and beat with a rolling pin until it is still cold but malleable, not soft or greasy. Shape into an even 6- by 6-inch (15 by 15 cm) square about 1/4 inch (1/2 cm) thick. Wrap in plastic and place in the refrigerator next to the dough for half an hour (no longer). The base dough and the butter should be about the same texture.

Single Turn

Turns

6 On a lightly floured surface, roll the 4 corners of the dough to form a rough square, keeping the centre thicker than the corners.

7 Place the butter square in the opposite direction of the square of dough (diamond in a square, see photo).

8 Wrap the butter in the dough, as if the dough is the envelope and the butter is a letter.

9 Place the dough package seam side up and begin to push down on the square with your rolling pin in both directions. Begin rolling starting from the centre point in both directions.

10 When the dough reaches about 18- by 10-inch (45 by 25 cm), make a turn in the dough by folding into thirds.

11 Wrap well and refrigerate at least 4 hours.

12 Let the dough come to room temperature for 10 minutes before beginning to roll. Roll the dough into a rectangle slightly longer than the first time. Fold both ends of the dough to meet each other in the centre. Then fold in half again. This is a double turn.

13 Wrap and refrigerate once again. Repeat both single and double turns again, each time wrapping the dough well and chilling for 4 hours between turns.

14 After the last turn, chill another 4 hours before use. The turns completed should be a single, then a double, a single, then a double. You can mark the dough with your fingertips to keep track as you go along. One indentation indicates a single turn, two a double.

Double Turn

Makes 3 lbs (1.5 kg) puff pastry

Storage: Wrap well.
Refrigerator: 2 days.
Freezer: Up to 6 weeks.

Egg Wash

Egg wash is a glaze used to give baked dough a golden colour and shine.

2 eggs 2
2 tablespoons milk **30 mL**
Pinch salt

1. Whisk all the ingredients together and strain before using.
2. Keep refrigerated when not in use.

Choux Pastry

Crispy on the outside and hollow on the inside, this dough is cooked twice: once on the stovetop and once in the oven.

Choux Pastry ~ Pâte à choux

INGREDIENTS

4 eggs **4**
1/2 cup water **125 mL**
1/2 cup milk **125 mL**
7 tablespoons unsalted butter **100 g**
1/2 teaspoon salt **3 g**
1 teaspoon sugar **7 g**
1 cup all-purpose flour **150 g**

METHOD

Preheat oven to 375°F (190°C). Prepare a parchment-lined baking sheet.

1 Crack the eggs into a large measuring cup and whisk until smooth.

2 In a medium-sized pot, bring the water, milk, butter, salt and sugar to a boil, stirring from time to time.

3 Add the flour all at once. Stir with a wooden spoon until it forms a thick, pasty dough.

4 Reduce to medium heat and stir the mixture vigorously until it begins to stick to the bottom of the pot and pull away from the sides.

5 Transfer the dough to a medium-sized bowl and begin stirring in the whisked eggs, about two tablespoons at a time, only adding more egg when the mixture is homogenous.

6 Check consistency of the dough before adding the fourth egg. It should be shiny and smooth yet hold its shape and not be runny.

7 Fill a pastry bag with the dough and pipe desired shapes onto a parchment paper.

8 Brush with egg wash. Bake for approximately 30 minutes or until the pastry is deep golden brown and well puffed.

9 Let cool to room temperature before filling.

Cooking hint: When the choux pastry is cooked, it will not crackle when held next to your ear. Storage: Wrap well. The baked dough can be frozen for up to 2 months.

Makes about 50 choux pastries

Basic Cakes

Basic Cakes

Techniques and Tips
Genoise
Chocolate Jelly Roll Cake
Sponge Cake
Ladyfingers
Chocolate Almond Cake
French Meringue
Meringue Mushrooms

Techniques and Tips

Techniques and Tips

- Always preheat your oven.
- Be careful not to overmix the batter when folding in the flour. The resulting cake will be heavy.
- Be sure to sift the dry ingredients.
- For even cooking, bake cakes in the middle of the oven.
- Do not move cakes or open the oven for the first 20 minutes while they are baking.
- Never cut a cake until it has completely cooled.
- Cakes are best made the day before they are to be served. They will slice more smoothly, resulting in fewer crumbs.
- Always defrost a frozen cake before cutting into layers.
- Keep cakes wrapped in plastic to keep them from drying out.
- To avoid soggy cakes, defrost a sponge cake in its plastic wrapping.

Buttering and flouring a cake mould

- Trace and cut a round parchment paper to fit in the base of the pan.
- Using a pastry brush, apply a thin layer of melted butter inside the mould.
- Place a circle of parchment paper in the base of the mould.
- Brush the paper with butter.
- Sprinkle the buttered mould with flour.
- Knock out the excess flour.

This recipe can easily be halved but since the baked cakes freeze well, it is worth making two at a time.

Genoise

INGREDIENTS

8 eggs **8**

1 1/4 cups granulated sugar **250 g**

1 2/3 cups all-purpose flour **250 g**

METHOD

Preheat oven to 350°F (180°C). Butter and flour two 8-inch (20 cm) round cake pans.

1. Sift the flour onto a piece of parchment paper.
2. In a medium-sized bowl, whisk the eggs and sugar together until well blended.
3. Set the bowl over a pot of rapidly boiling water (bain-marie) and whisk the mixture until warm to the touch.
4. With an electric mixer, beat the mixture at high speed for 5 minutes until it has tripled in volume. Reduce the mixer speed to medium and beat for a further 5 minutes. The mixture should reach ribbon consistency: a thick foam that keeps its shape when it falls from the whisk.
5. Gently fold the flour into the egg mixture, 1 tablespoon at a time, with a large rubber spatula. Do not overmix or the batter will fall.
6. Pour the mixture into the prepared pans and immediately place in the preheated oven.
7. Bake for about 25 minutes or until the cakes bounce back when pressed and begin to pull away from the sides of the pans.
8. Let cool 10 minutes. Unmould and cool on a rack.

For Chocolate Genoise: *Replace 1/4 cup (35 g) of flour with 1/4 cup (25 g) sifted cocoa powder.*

Makes two 8-inch (20 cm) cakes
Storage: Wrap well.
Freezer: Up to 1 month.

This sheet of cake is flexible enough to be rolled for cakes such as the bûche de Noël.

Chocolate Jelly Roll Cake

INGREDIENTS

1/4 cup all-purpose flour **40 g**
1/3 cup cocoa powder **30 g**
3 large eggs **3**
3 large eggs, separated **3**
3/4 cup granulated sugar **150 g**
Pinch salt

METHOD

Preheat oven to 375°F (190°C). Line a lightly greased 17- by 11-inch (42 by 28 cm) jelly roll pan with a sheet of parchment paper.

1. Sift the flour and cocoa powder onto the parchment paper. In a large bowl, using an electric mixer, beat together eggs, egg yolks, 1/2 cup (100 g) sugar and salt for 5 minutes on high speed. Continue beating for another 5 minutes at medium speed until the mixture is very frothy and has more than doubled in volume.
2. In a separate clean bowl, beat the whites with an electric mixer at high speed, gradually adding the remaining 1/4 cup sugar (50 g), until they hold soft peaks.
3. With a rubber spatula, fold the whites into the beaten yolk mixture and then carefully fold in the flour a couple of tablespoons at a time.
4. Spread the mixture evenly onto the prepared pan and bake for about 15 minutes or until the cake springs back to the touch. Let cool completely on a rack.
5. Unmould the sheet cake by running a serrated knife around the edges and, with the help of the paper, lift it out of the pan.

Makes one 17- by 11-inch (42 by 28 cm) sheet cake

Storage: Wrap well. Refrigerator: 2 days.
Freezer: Up to 6 weeks.

For a White Jelly Roll Cake: *Replace the amount of flour and cocoa powder with 1/2 cup (75 g) all-purpose flour.*

This is a very simple French sponge cake that is delicious paired with a custard sauce or fruit. It is important not to overbeat the whites or the cake will not rise properly. This cake can be made in either a decorative mould or a regular cake pan. It can be used in place of a genoise.

Sponge Cake ~ Gâteau de Savoie

Ingredients

4 egg yolks **4**
3/4 cup granulated sugar **150 g**
1/3 cup all-purpose flour **50 g**
1/2 cup cornstarch **55 g**
1 tablespoon Grand Marnier *or* orange juice **15 mL**
2 teaspoons vanilla extract **10 mL**
4 egg whites **4**
Pinch salt

Icing sugar for decoration

Method

Preheat oven to 350°F (180°C). Butter and lightly flour an 8-inch (20 cm) decorative cake mould or bundt pan.

1. Sift the flour and cornstarch together onto a piece of parchment paper.
2. In a large bowl, beat the egg yolks with 1/2 cup (125 g) of the sugar until very light and fluffy. Stir in the vanilla and Grand Marnier, followed by the flour and cornstarch. You will end up with a thick paste. Do not overwork.
3. Beat the egg whites, remaining sugar and the pinch of salt on low speed until frothy. Gradually increase the speed to high until the mixture forms soft peaks.
4. Whisk one third of the whites into the base mixture until well combined and fold in the rest with a rubber spatula.
5. Pour the mixture into the prepared mould and bake in the preheated oven for 30 minutes or until the sponge springs back when pressed.
6. Unmould onto a metal rack while still warm. Let cool and sprinkle the top of the cake with sifted icing sugar.

Makes one 8-inch (20 cm) cake
Storage: Wrap well. Refrigerator: 2 days. Freezer: Up to 6 weeks

Used to enclose the Vanilla Berry Charlotte (p.77) these ladyfingers are piped closely together in bands to facilitate lining the mould. The remaining batter is piped into two 7-inch (18 cm) rounds which will be placed at the base and the middle of the charlotte. This cake is sprinkled with two coats of icing sugar to create the desired sugary crust. Ladyfingers can also be piped into individual soft cookies that are often served with Champagne.

Ladyfingers ~ Doigts de dame

INGREDIENTS

5 egg whites **5**
1/2 cup and 2 tablespoons granulated sugar **125 g**
5 egg yolks **5**
2/3 cup and 2 tablespoons all-purpose flour **120 g**
Icing sugar

METHOD

Preheat oven to 400°F (200°C). Prepare a pastry bag with a 3/4-inch (15mm) tip. Prepare 2 sheets of parchment paper to fit 2 standard cookie sheets (11- by 17-inches / 28 by 42 cm). With a pencil, trace 3 bands along the long side (horizontal) of the paper, 3 1/2 inches (8 cm) apart. Using an 8-inch (20 cm) mould to guide you, trace two circles on the second sheet of parchment. Turn both sheets, pencil mark side down, onto the baking sheets.

1. Sift the flour onto a piece of parchment paper.
2. In a medium-sized, very clean stainless steel bowl, beat the egg whites with an electric mixer at high speed, adding the sugar gradually, 1 tablespoon at a time.
3. Continue beating on high speed until the mixture forms very stiff peaks.
4. Quickly add the yolks, beat for 2 seconds and immediately turn off the machine.

5 With a large rubber spatula, fold the flour into the mixture.

6 Fill the pastry bag with the mixture.

7 Following the traced lines, pipe the ladyfingers onto the parchment, so that they barely touch one another. Pipe the remaining batter in a spiral round, 1-inch (2.5 cm) within the inside of the traced circles.

8 When all the mixture has been piped, sprinkle a thin layer of icing sugar over the entire surface of the bands of ladyfingers and the rounds. Wait 5 minutes and sprinkle a second coat.

9 Bake until they just begin to colour, about 10 minutes.

10 Let cool completely before peeling off the parchment.

Makes enough lady fingers to line and fill one 8-inch (20 cm) charlotte cake
Storage: Wrap well. Freezer: 6 weeks.

This rich almond-flavoured chocolate cake is the one used to make a high quality chocolate cake such as the Triple Chocolat Almond Cake (p.72).

Chocolate Almond Cake

INGREDIENTS

- **1/4 cup** butter, melted **50 mL**
- **1/2 cup** cocoa powder **50 g**
- **1/2 cup** cornstarch **55 g**
- **7 oz** almond paste **210 g**
- **6** egg yolks **6**
- **1 1/4 cups** icing sugar **140 g**
- **2** eggs **2**
- **6** egg whites **6**
- **1/3 cup** granulated sugar **70 g**

METHOD

Preheat oven to 350°F (180°C). Butter two 9-inch (23 cm) cake moulds, line the base with a circle of parchment paper, butter again and flour the moulds.

1. Sift together the cornstarch and the cocoa powder. Melt the butter and allow to cool to room temperature.
2. In a large bowl, with the paddle attachment of a mixer or an electric beater on low speed, blend together the almond paste, the icing sugar and the egg yolks, one by one, followed by the eggs, scraping down the sides as you go, ensuring that the mixture is homogenous.
3. In a medium-sized bowl with an electric mixer, beat the egg whites at high speed, gradually adding the granulated sugar until they form soft but firm peaks.
4. Fold the beaten egg whites gently into the almond mixture, followed by the dry ingredients and finally the melted butter.
5. Pour the batter into the prepared moulds and place them in the preheated oven for 45 minutes or until a tester comes out clean.

Makes two 9-inch (23 cm) cakes
Storage: Wrap well.
Refrigerator: 2 days.
Freezer: Up to 6 weeks

This hard meringue is ideal for making small cookies or trompe l'œil mushrooms, which are the perfect decoration for the Bûche de Noël or a whimsical addition to a platter of Christmas cookies.

French Meringue

French Meringue

INGREDIENTS

2 egg whites **2**
5 tablespoons granulated sugar **60 g**
1/2 cup sifted icing sugar **55 g**
1/2 teaspoon almond extract **2 mL**
1/2 teaspoon vanilla extract **2 mL**

METHOD

Preheat oven to 200°F (100°C).

1. With an electric mixer at high speed, beat the egg whites until they are foamy and begin to whiten.
2. Gradually add the granulated sugar a tablespoon at a time and continue beating until the whites hold very stiff, glossy peaks.
3. With a clean rubber spatula, fold in the icing sugar a tablespoon at a time, and finally the extracts.
4. Pipe into desired shape.

Meringue Mushrooms

1. Set aside about 1/4 cup (50 mL) of meringue, covered.
2. With a pastry bag fitted with a 1/2-inch (1 cm) round tip, pipe out caps and stems of the mushrooms separately onto parchment-lined baking sheets.
3. Sift some cocoa power onto the mushroom caps and bake in a warm oven until firm and dry, about 3 hours. Turn off the oven and let cool completely in the turned-off oven.
4. Using the reserved meringue, stick together the stems and caps and re-bake the whole mushrooms in a 200°F (100°C) oven for another 1/2 hour. Keep stored in an airtight container until ready to use.

Make about 30 mushrooms.
Storage: Meringues must be stored in an airtight container at room temperature. They must never be refrigerated.

Creams, Fillings and Sauces

Creams, Fillings and Sauces

Chantilly Cream
Pastry Cream
Light Cream
Buttercream
Mousseline Cream
Almond Cream
Lemon Curd
Classic Ganache
Ganache Icing
Custard Cream
Caramel Sauce
Chocolate Sauce
Applesauce
Fruit Coulis
Simple Fruit Mousse
Vanilla Bavarian
Chocolate Mousse

Not simply whipped cream, Chantilly is a sweetened and flavoured cream used to garnish and fill pastries, cakes and desserts.

Chantilly Cream

INGREDIENTS

2 cups 35% cream **500 mL**
1/4 cup granulated sugar **50 g**
1 teaspoon vanilla extract **5 mL**

Makes 2 cups (500 mL)
Storage: Wrap well. Refrigerator: No longer than 1 day.

METHOD

1 Refrigerate a mixing bowl and beaters for 15 minutes before proceeding.

2 Whisk together all ingredients in the chilled bowl and beat with an electric mixer on medium speed until the cream holds stiff peaks.

3 Keep refrigerated and well covered until ready to use.

Pastry Cream ~ Crème Pâtissière

This cooked cream is used in many French cakes and pastries.

INGREDIENTS

1 cup milk **250 mL**
1 teaspoon vanilla extract **5 mL**
1/4 cup granulated sugar **50 g**
3 egg yolks **3**
2 1/2 tablespoons cornstarch **18 g**
1 teaspoon unsalted butter **4 g**

METHOD

1 In a small saucepan, bring the milk, vanilla and half the sugar to a boil.

2 Meanwhile, in a small bowl, beat the yolks vigorously with the remaining sugar until well combined. Add the cornstarch and whisk until very smooth.

3 Pour a third of the boiling milk into the yolk mixture and whisk until smooth.

4 Pour the diluted egg mixture back into the saucepan of milk and, over high heat, continue whisking constantly until it begins to boil. Whisk and boil for a full 30 seconds. Whisk in the butter.

5 Transfer the cream to a clean shallow bowl, cover immediately with plastic wrap and place in the refrigerator until cool.

Makes 1 1/2 cups (375 mL)
Storage: Refrigerator: 5 days. Not to be frozen.

Light Cream

This cream consists of pastry cream lightened by the addition of Chantilly. It is the ideal filling for fruit tarts.

Light Cream ~ Crème légère

INGREDIENTS

1 recipe pastry cream (p. 32) **1**

1/2 recipe Chantilly cream (p. 32) **1/2**

3 tablespoons of flavouring such as kirsch, Grand Marnier or rum **45 mL**

METHOD

1 In a medium-sized bowl, whisk the cold pastry cream until it is smooth and lump-free. Whisk in a third of the Chantilly and, with a rubber spatula, gently fold in the remaining Chantilly cream and the flavouring.

Makes 2 cups (500 mL)
Storage: Wrap well.
Refrigerator: 1 day.
Not to be frozen.

Buttercream

Buttercream is an essential ingredient in cake making. When properly made, it should not be too heavy or sweet.

Buttercream

INGREDIENTS

1 3/4 cups granulated sugar **350 g**
3/4 cup water **175 mL**
5 egg yolks **5**
2 eggs **2**
3 cups unsalted butter, room temperature **680 g**
1 to 1 1/2 tablespoons vanilla extract **15 to 22 mL**

Makes 6 1/2 cups (1,6 L)

METHOD

1. In a small very clean saucepan, combine the water and sugar and bring to a boil over high heat. When the syrup begins to boil, brush the sides with a clean, wet pastry brush to avoid the accumulation of sugar crystals.
2. Clip a candy thermometer to the side of the pot and continue to boil until the syrup reaches 250°F (120°C).
3. In a medium-sized bowl, with an electric mixer, beat the yolks and eggs on high speed until fluffy.
4. Begin pouring the hot sugar syrup in a fine stream over the yolks, beating constantly on high speed.
5. Once all the syrup has been poured, continue beating the mixture for 5 minutes on high speed, then reduce to medium speed and beat until the mixture is room temperature (cool to the touch).
6. Begin blending in the butter a few tablespoons at a time and continue beating at high speed until the cream is completely smooth, white in colour, and holds a stiff peak. Beat in the vanilla.

Storage: Wrap well. Refrigerator: 1 week. Freezer: 6 weeks.

This rich cream is a cross between buttercream and pastry cream. It must be used immediately since it hardens when chilled.

Mousseline Cream

Mousseline Cream

INGREDIENTS

1 1/2 cups milk **375 mL**
3/4 cup granulated sugar **150 g**
1 egg **1**
1 egg yolk **1**
1/3 cup cornstarch **40 g**
3/4 cup unsalted butter, room temperature **170 g**

METHOD

1. In a large saucepan, bring the milk and half the sugar to a boil.
2. Meanwhile, in a small bowl, beat the egg and egg yolk vigorously with the remaining sugar until well combined. Add the cornstarch and whisk until very smooth.
3. Pour one third of the boiling milk into the egg mixture and whisk until smooth.
4. Pour the diluted egg mixture back into the saucepan of milk and, over high heat, continue whisking constantly until it begins to boil. Whisk and boil for a full 30 seconds. Whisk in half the butter.
5. Transfer the cream to a clean shallow bowl, cover immediately with plastic wrap and place in the refrigerator. Chill overnight.
6. Remove the cream from the refrigerator for 15 minutes. It must be at room temperature before proceeding with the recipe.
7. In a medium-sized bowl, with an electric mixer, beat the cream until smooth. Begin blending in the butter a few tablespoons at a time and continue beating at high speed until the cream is completely smooth and holds a stiff peak.
8. Use immediately as required.

Makes about 3 cups (750 mL)

This cream is meant to be cooked. It will form a cake-like layer on the base of a tart.

Almond Cream

Almond Cream

INGREDIENTS

6 tablespoons unsalted butter **80 g**
3/4 cup powdered almonds **90 g**
6 tablespoons granulated sugar **75 g**
2 eggs **2**
2 tablespoons flour **20 g**
1 teaspoon vanilla extract **5 mL**
1/2 teaspoon almond extract **2 mL**

METHOD

1 In a medium-sized bowl, with an electric mixer, beat the butter at high speed until smooth and creamy, followed by the sugar and powdered almonds.

2 Beat in the eggs and the flour and finally the vanilla and almond extracts.

3 Use immediately or store, well-wrapped, in the refrigerator.

Makes 1 1/3 cups (325 mL)
Storage: Wrap well. Refrigerator: 4 days.

This tangy lemon cream is used to make lemon tarts. It's also a great filling for fruit tarts — just follow the recipe for light cream (page 34), substituting the lemon curd for the pastry cream.

Lemon Curd

Lemon Curd ~ CRÈME AU CITRON

INGREDIENTS

1 cup freshly squeezed lemon juice **250 mL**
Zest of 3 lemons
1 1/4 cups granulated sugar **250 g**
1 cup unsalted butter **210 g**
4 eggs **4**
4 egg yolks **4**

METHOD

1. In a medium-sized non-reactive saucepan, bring the lemon juice, zest, half the sugar and half the butter to a boil over high heat.
2. Meanwhile, in a small bowl, beat the eggs and egg yolks vigorously with the remaining sugar until well combined.
3. Pour one third of the boiling lemon juice into the egg mixture and whisk until smooth.
4. Pour the diluted egg mixture back into the saucepan, reduce the heat to medium and stir the mixture constantly until it has thickened enough to coat the back of a spoon. Whisk in the remaining butter, a tablespoon at a time, until the mixture is very thick, shiny and smooth. At no point should the mixture come to a boil.
5. Either pour the cream immediately into a 9-inch (23 cm) baked tart shell or transfer the cream to a clean shallow bowl, cover immediately with plastic wrap and place in the refrigerator. Chill overnight.

Makes 3 1/2 cups (875 mL)

Storage: In an airtight container.
Refrigerator: 1 week.
Freezer: Up to 2 weeks.

Ganache can be used for many purposes: in its liquid form as a glaze, as a base for chocolate truffles or as a filling for cakes and pastries.

Classic Ganache

Classic Ganache

INGREDIENTS

6 oz bittersweet or semisweet chocolate, finely chopped **170 g**
3/4 cup 35% cream **185 mL**

METHOD

1 Chop the chocolate into very small pieces and place in a medium-sized bowl.

2 In a small saucepan, bring the cream to a boil. Pour half of the cream over the chocolate and stir with a wooden spoon or rubber spatula.

3 When the mixture is smooth, gradually stir in the remaining cream, a bit at a time. Continue stirring until the mixture is smooth and shiny and all the chocolate has completely melted.

Makes about 1 1/2 cups (375 mL)
Storage: Wrap well. Refrigerator: 1 week.

Ganache Icing

This is a rich, heavy icing that shouldn't be too fluffy.

INGREDIENTS

1 recipe ganache (above) **1**

1/4 cup icing sugar **37 g**

1/4 cup unsalted butter, room temperature **55 g**

METHOD

1 Leave the ganache at room temperature until it is set through (about 2 hours in a cool place, not the refrigerator).

2 In a medium-sized bowl with an electric mixer, blend the butter and icing sugar into the ganache and beat until the icing is smooth and just holds its shape.

Makes about 2 1/4 cups (550 mL)

Custard Cream ~ Crème anglaise

Custard Cream

INGREDIENTS

2 cups milk **500 mL**
2 teaspoons vanilla extract **10 mL**
1/2 cup granulated sugar **100 g**
5 egg yolks **5**

METHOD

1. Prepare an ice bath, a clean medium-sized bowl and a fine strainer.
2. In a medium-sized saucepan, bring the milk, vanilla and half the sugar to a boil.
3. Meanwhile, in a small bowl, beat the yolks vigorously with the remaining sugar until well combined.
4. Pour a third of the boiling milk into the yolk mixture and whisk until smooth.
5. Pour the diluted egg mixture back into the saucepan of milk. Reduce the heat to low. Place a candy thermometer in the mixture and continue heating, whisking all the while, until the mixture reaches 185°F (85°C).
6. Immediately strain the cream into the prepared bowl and cool over an ice bath.
7. Cover with plastic wrap and refrigerate.

Makes 2 1/2 cups (625 mL)
Storage: Refrigerator: 3 days.

Caramel Sauce

INGREDIENTS

1 1/4 cups granulated sugar **250 g**
1/4 cup white corn syrup **55 g**
1 tablespoon butter **14 g**
1 1/4 cups 35% cream **310 mL**
1 teaspoon vanilla extract **5 mL**
Pinch salt

METHOD

1 Place sugar and corn syrup in a clean small pot over medium heat.

2 Stir until it turns a deep caramel colour.

3 Remove from heat and add the butter. Gradually whisk in the cream and vanilla.

4 Bring back to a boil for a few minutes. Strain and let cool.

5 Serve at room temperature.

Makes 1 1/2 cups (375 mL)

Chocolate Sauce

INGREDIENTS

1 cup milk **250 mL**

2 tablespoons white corn syrup *or* honey **30 mL**

7 oz semisweet chocolate **210 g**

METHOD

1 Chop the chocolate into small pieces and place in a medium-sized bowl.

2 In a small saucepan, bring the milk and corn syrup to a boil. Pour half the milk mixture over the chocolate and stir with a wooden spoon or a rubber spatula. When the mixture is smooth, gradually stir in the remaining milk mixture, a bit at a time.

3 Serve warm.

Makes 1 1/2 cups (375 mL)

Applesauce

Applesauce has many uses. In pastry, it is often used as a base for French apple tarts.

INGREDIENTS

1 pound apples, about 6 apples **454 g**

3/4 cup granulated sugar **150 g**

2 cups water **500 mL**

1 vanilla bean or **2 teaspoons** vanilla extract **10 mL**

1 cinnamon stick or **1/2 teaspoon** cinnamon **2 g**

METHOD

1 Peel, seed and core the apples and dice into large cubes.

2 In a large pot, combine the sugar, water, apple pieces and spices.

3 Cook over medium-low heat for 20 minutes, stirring often or until most of the water has evaporated. Remove from heat and let cool to room temperature.

4 Remove the cinnamon stick and vanilla bean and force through a sieve or a food mill into a clean shallow bowl. Cover with plastic wrap and refrigerate.

Makes about 1 1/2 cups (375 mL)
Storage: Refrigerator: 1 week. Can be frozen but not recommended.

Fruit Coulis

INGREDIENTS

1 lb fresh fruit, such as strawberries, raspberries, mango or kiwi **500 g**

Juice of 1 lemon

1/4 cup sugar **50 g**

1 tablespoon Kirsch *or* other alcohol (optional) **15 mL**

METHOD

1. Wash the fruit if necessary.
2. Remove the stems and/or skins.
3. Cut the fruit into small pieces. Stir in the lemon juice, sugar and alcohol. Cover and refrigerate overnight.
4. Puree in a blender or food processor until smooth and strain to remove any seeds.
5. Adjust sweetness if necessary.

Makes about 1 3/4 cups (440 mL)
Storage: Refrigerator: Up to 3 days. Freezer: 6 weeks.

If the fruit coulis is made with very sweet, ripe fruit, the icing sugar can be omitted. This mousse can be used to fill a charlotte cake instead of the Vanilla Bavarian.

Simple Fruit Mousse

INGREDIENTS

5 gelatin leaves or **2 1/2 teaspoons** powdered gelatin **9 g**
2 cups 35% cream **500 mL**
2 tablespoons icing sugar **14 g**
1 cup fruit coulis, room temperature **250 mL**

METHOD

1. Soak the gelatin leaves one by one in a small bowl of cold water; set aside. If using powdered gelatin, sprinkle it over 5 tablespoons (75 mL) of water to let it soften.
2. In a small bowl, with an electric mixer, whip the 35% cream with the icing sugar to very soft peaks and refrigerate.
3. Remove the softened gelatin leaves from their bowl, squeeze out the excess water and melt them in a small plastic container in the microwave (20 seconds on high heat) or in a small metal bowl over a pot of boiling water (bain-marie). The gelatin should not be hot, just warm. If using powdered, melt the softened mixture using the same method.
4. Pour a third of the coulis into the warm gelatin. Whisk in the remaining coulis and a third of the whipped cream. Fold in the remaining cream and pour into a serving bowl, individual dessert cups or moulded cake.
5. Chill at least 6 hours before serving.

Makes 3 cups (750 mL)

Bavarian cream is similar to a mousse but the base is a gelatinized custard cream instead of a fruit purée. Be sure not to overcook the base custard or your Bavarian will not be smooth.

Vanilla Bavarian

INGREDIENTS

1 1/3 cups milk **330 mL**
2 teaspoons vanilla extract **10 mL** *or* **1/2** vanilla bean
1/2 cup granulated sugar **100 g**
4 egg yolks **4**
3 gelatin leaves or **2 teaspoons** powdered gelatin **7 g**
1 2/3 cups 35% cream **410 mL**

METHOD

1. Soak the gelatin leaves one by one in a small bowl of cold water; set aside. If using powdered gelatin, sprinkle it over 1/4 cup (50 mL) of cold water to let it soften.
2. In a small bowl, with an electric mixer, whip the 35% cream to very soft peaks and refrigerate.
3. Prepare an ice bath, a clean medium-sized bowl and a fine strainer.
4. In a medium-sized saucepan, bring the milk, vanilla and half the sugar to a boil.
5. Meanwhile, in a small bowl, beat the yolks vigorously with the remaining sugar until well combined.
6. Pour one third of the boiling milk into the yolk mixture and whisk until smooth.
7. Pour the diluted egg mixture back into the saucepan of milk. Turn the heat to low. Place a candy thermometer in the mixture and continue heating, whisking all the while, until the mixture reaches 185°F (85°C). Remove from the heat.
8. Immediately strain the cream into the prepared bowl. Remove the softened gelatin leaves from their bowl, squeeze out the excess water and whisk them into the custard mixture. If using powdered gelatin, whisk the softened gelatin into the hot custard.
9. Place the bowl over an ice bath, stirring slowly and constantly until the mixture begins to thicken.
10. Immediately whisk a third of the whipped cream into the mixture. Fold in the remainder of the cream with a rubber spatula.
11. Pour into dessert cups or into a charlotte cake.

Makes about 3 cups (750 mL), enough to fill an 8-inch (20 cm) charlotte

When making chocolate mousse, do not refrigerate your heavy cream after it has been whipped or the resulting mousse will be too thick. Also, the better quality chocolate you use, the richer and more delicious the final product will be.

Chocolate Mousse

INGREDIENTS

1/4 cup sugar **50 g**

1/4 cup water **50 mL**

3 egg yolks **3**

6 oz semisweet chocolate **180 g**

1 1/2 cups 35% cream **375 mL**

METHOD

1. In a small bowl, with an electric mixer, whip the 35% cream to very soft peaks.

2. Prepare a small pot of simmering water over low heat. Chop the chocolate into small pieces and place in a small stainless steel bowl. Place the bowl over the pot of simmering water to melt the chocolate, stirring often, over medium heat, until very warm to the touch. Set aside.

3. In a small stainless steel bowl, vigorously whisk together the egg yolks, sugar and water until well blended. Place this bowl over the simmering water and whisk the mixture by hand until it turns from a liquid state into a thick mousse. Remove from heat.

4. With an electric hand mixer, beat on high speed until cool. It should be creamy and double in volume.

5. Pour a third of the whipped cream into the warm chocolate and whisk until thoroughly blended. Fold in the yolk mixture with a rubber spatula, followed by the remaining cream. Fold until just combined.

6. Pour into a decorative serving bowl or use to make the chocolate mousse cake on p. 79. Chill 6 hours before serving.

Makes about 3 cups (750 mL), enough mousse for an 8-inch (20 cm) chocolate mousse cake

Pies and Tarts

Pies and Tarts

Technique and Tips
Apple Pie
French Apple Tart
Tarte Tatin
Apricot Glaze
Poached Pears
Pear or Apricot Almond Tart
Fruit Tart
Lemon Tart
Maple Pie and Pecan Pie
Chocolate Tart

Rolling pastry

Techniques and Tips

Techniques and Tips

Pastry can be formed into many different shapes and sizes. Experiment with square pans, rectangular pans and individual tartlets.

Rolling pastry and lining a tart mould

1. Cut the cold dough into small pieces. Warm the pieces by squeezing each piece in your hand. Press the pieces together.
2. Form the dough into a thin round disk, turning the edges under to form a smooth border.
3. Lightly flour the work table and the top of your dough.
4. Press down on your dough with your rolling pin from the centre to the sides.
5. Begin rolling the dough, always rolling out (up or down) from the centre. Turn the dough every three or four rolls to help form a circle and keep it from sticking to the work surface. Add more flour as needed, but avoid adding too much flour which, when absorbed by the dough, will make the crust tough.
6. If the dough cracks, just press it back into shape. If it forms a hole, patch with an extra piece of dough.
7. Dough rolled for tart bases should be no thicker than 1/16 inch (about 3 mm). If your pastry becomes too soft to manage, roll it onto a baking sheet and chill until firm.
8. Roll the dough onto your rolling pin and unroll it over your mould.
9. Lift the sides of the dough and press it firmly into the corners of the mould.
10. Fold the overhanging dough to form a ridge along the top of the mould. Press the ridge up to form a border of pastry along the top of the mould. Refrigerate at least 30 minutes before baking.

Preparing a sweet pastry base using the grating method

Cold sweet pastry can be grated on a box grater and pressed into the sides and bottom of a tart shell.

Blind baking

Making a tart shell using a puff pastry

Blind baking shortcrust pastry and sweet pastry shells:

1. Preheat oven to 375°F (190°C).
2. With a fork, poke holes all over the bottom surface of the raw tart shell (docking). Line it with a large circle of parchment paper and fill with metal baking weights, dry beans or rice to hold down the crust.
3. Bake the shell for 15 minutes or until the tart rim begins to colour. Remove from oven. Remove the paper and beans and bake again until the base is cooked and begins to colour.
4. Remove from oven and let cool completely on a rack.

Making a tart shell using puff pastry

A puff pastry tart shell can be used in place of a sweet shell when making a fruit tart (jardinière).

1. Place the square block of cold puff pastry on a large floured surface. With a rolling pin, press the pastry down from top to bottom. Turn the pastry a quarter turn and press down in the other direction. Continue this motion until the pastry is flat enough to be rolled.
2. Roll the pastry in both directions into a rectangular shape which is about a third longer than wide. The thickness of the dough should be equal to that of two coins stacked on top of each other, about 1/8 inch (3 mm).
3. With a large sharp chef's knife or pizza cutter, and with the help of a ruler, straighten out the sides, removing as little pastry as possible. Cut a 1 inch (2.5 cm) band off the four sides of the dough and set aside. Cut the remaining dough into the size you want your tart to be. Fold it in half and transfer it to a baking sheet. With a fork, poke holes in the entire surface of the pastry.
4. Brush all four sides of the tart with water and stick the 1-inch (2.5 cm) bands on top of the base, 1/4 inch (6 mm) from the edge. The base is now flat, but when baked it will look like a box. Wrap and chill the tart base for at least 30 minutes.

Baking a puff pastry tart shell

1. Preheat oven to 400°F (200°C).
2. Remove the tart base from the refrigerator and brush some egg wash on the side bands.
3. Bake for about 30 minutes or until the shell is a deep golden colour. Remove from oven and let cool on a rack until the tart base has cooled.

This is the traditional North American apple pie. Be sure to use cooking apples such as Golden Delicious, Granny Smith, Cortland, or a combination of all three, which hold their shape when baked.

Apple Pie

INGREDIENTS

Filling

8 baking apples **8**

Juice of 1 lemon

1/2 to 2/3 cup granulated sugar **100 g to 140 g**

Pinch salt

3 tablespoons butter **43 g**

1 vanilla bean, split and scraped **1**

1 cinnamon stick **1**

1 tablespoon cornstarch **7 g**

3 tablespoons water **45 mL**

1 recipe shortcrust pastry (p.14) **1**

Egg wash (p. 18)

2 tablespoons granulated sugar **25 g**

METHOD

Preheat oven to 425°F (220°C).
Prepare an ungreased 10 inch (25 cm), 1 1/2-inch (3.5 cm) deep pie plate.

1. Prepare filling. Peel and core the apples and cut them into 1 inch (2.5 cm) cubes. Place in a large bowl and stir in the lemon juice.
2. In a large frying pan, heat the sugar with the salt over high heat until it melts. Continue heating until it turns a deep caramel colour and begins to smoke. Turn off the heat and quickly stir in the butter and apples. Return to medium heat, add the vanilla bean and cinnamon stick. Simmer, stirring gently from time to time, until the apples are tender.
3. Strain the filling, catching the juices in a bowl underneath the strainer. Let drain until all the juices have seeped out. Pour the juices back in the frying pan off heat.
4. In a small bowl, whisk together the cornstarch and water. Heat the juice in the frying pan to a simmer and whisk in the cornstarch mixture. Bring to a boil for 10 seconds, whisking constantly, and remove from heat. The mixture should be a thick liquid. If too thick, thin out with a little water.
5. In a large bowl, combine the sautéed apples and thickened juices. Set aside.
6. Assemble the pie. Cut the dough in half and form each half into a flat disk. Roll each disk into 14 inch (35 cm) rounds, no thicker than 1/8th of an inch (3 mm). Line the pie plate with one of the rounds, making sure it fits well into the sides and bottom of the plate.
7. Pour the filling into the dough-lined pie plate, taking care to avoid spilling any of the juices on the rim of the dough.
8. Fold the other round into quarters, and cut 2 steam vents on an angle through the 2 layers of dough. Brush a thin layer of water on the rim of the filled base. Unfold the top layer and place on top of the apple layer. There should be dough hanging over all sides. Press to seal the dough where it meets at the rim of the pie plate. With a sharp knife, cut off the overhanging dough.
9. Brush the top of the pie with egg wash and sprinkle with sugar.
10. Place in preheated oven for 10 minutes, then turn the heat down to 375°F (190°C). Bake until the pie is deep golden and the juices are bubbling, about 30 more minutes.
11. Let cool on a rack before serving.

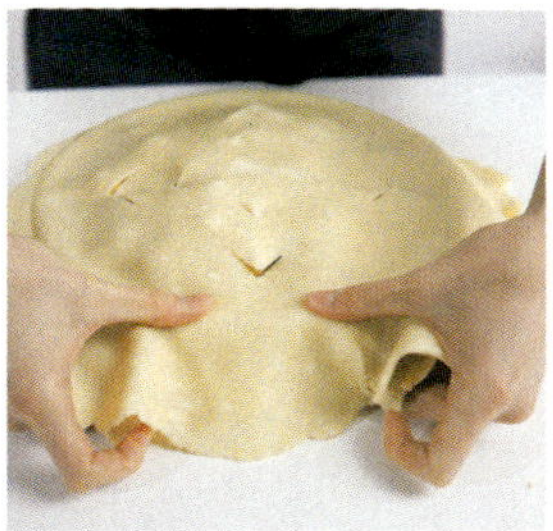

Makes one 10-inch (25 cm) tart, serving 8 persons

This single-crust apple tart is the one seen most frequently in French boulangeries and pâtisseries. It is quite easy to make — just take care to slice the apples as thin as possible and to place the slices evenly.

French Apple Tart

INGREDIENTS

1/2 recipe shortcrust pastry (p.14) 1/2
1 recipe applesauce (p.41) 1
4 large Golden Delicious, Cortland or Granny Smith apples 4
Egg wash (p.18)
Granulated sugar

METHOD

Preheat oven to 350°F (180°C).

1 Prepare tart base for a French-style single pie crust using shortcrust pastry (p.14).

2 Fill the shell halfway with applesauce.

3 Peel and core the apples, and slice in half vertically.

4 Lay each apple half flat on a cutting board; with a very sharp knife, cut the apple into thin slices.

5 Arrange the apples decoratively in spirals on top of the apple sauce.

6 Brush a thin layer of egg wash over the apples and sprinkle with a generous amount of sugar.

7 Bake until the apples and crust are golden.

8 Let cool to room temperature before slicing.

Makes one 9-inch (23 cm) tart, serving 8-10 persons

What distinguishes a Tarte Tatin from an apple tart with caramel is that it is cooked upside-down. This way, the juice from the apples seeps into the butter and sugar at the base of the pan, creating a perfumed and acidic caramel that the fruit eventually absorbs. A perfect tart will be deep golden and glossy, with a little extra juice. We added the step of caramelizing the sugar before baking the tart for an even richer caramel colour and flavour.

Tarte Tatin

INGREDIENTS

1 half-recipe shortcrust pastry (p. 14) **1**
10-12 Golden Delicious, Cortland or Granny Smith apples **10-12**
2 tablespoons lemon juice **30 mL**
3/4 cup granulated sugar **150 g**
Pinch salt
4 tablespoons cold unsalted butter, cut into pieces **55 g**

METHOD

Preheat oven to 375°F (190°C). Prepare a 9-inch (23 cm), 3-inch (7.5 cm) deep cake pan.

1. Roll the dough out on a floured surface to 1/8-inch (3 mm) thickness. Cut a 10-inch (25 cm) circle in the rolled dough, a bit larger than the base of your baking pan. Place the pastry on a baking sheet and chill while you prepare the apples.
2. Peel and core the apples and cut them in half. In a large bowl, toss the apple pieces with the lemon juice to prevent them from turning brown.
3. Sprinkle half the sugar with the pinch of salt evenly over the bottom of the pan and heat on the stove over medium heat until the sugar turns an even golden colour. Immediately remove from the burner and stir in half the butter. Let cool until the caramel begins to thicken.
4. Arrange the apple halves upright in tight concentric circles. Sprinkle with the remaining sugar and add the remaining butter in knobs over the surface of the apples. Set aside.
5. Top the apples with the chilled pastry, pressing it gently onto the apples, and tuck in any overhanging edges.
6. Bake for 1 hour or until the pastry is golden and baked through.
7. To unmould, let the tart cool completely on a rack. Place a serving dish on top, then quickly turn the tart upside down. Remove the pan. If a few pieces of apple stick to the tin, remove and carefully arrange them on the tart.

Makes one 9-inch (23 cm) tart, serving 8-10 persons

Serving tip: If you wish to serve the tart warm, re-heat only after it has cooled and unmoulded; otherwise it may be too runny.

Warm apricot glaze is brushed in a thin layer over fruit tarts.

Apricot Glaze

INGREDIENTS

1 cup apricot jelly **250 mL**
2 tablespoons water **30 mL**

METHOD

1 Combine the apricot jelly and water in a small saucepan, over low heat. Heat, whisking from time to time, until the jelly melts and the mixture begins to boil. Let the mixture reduce by one quarter. Strain and keep warm.

Poached Pears

INGREDIENTS

4 cups water **1 L**
1 1/4 cups sugar **250 g**
Juice of 1 lemon
4 large, ripe pears, peeled (leaving the stems on) **4**

METHOD

1 Pour the water into a large pot and whisk in the sugar. Add the lemon juice.

2 Place the peeled pears in the cold liquid and bring to a boil.

3 Immediately reduce the heat to a simmer, place a round of parchment paper over the exposed fruit and continue to cook until a paring knife easily pierces the pears, about 15 minutes.

4 Remove from stove and let pears cool in poaching syrup.

This tart is ideally made with fresh apricots or poached fresh pears, but canned fruit can be used in a pinch.

Pear or Apricot Almond Tart

Pear or Apricot Almond Tart

INGREDIENTS

1 unbaked sweetcrust pastry shell (9-inch or 23 cm) (p. 14) 1

1 recipe almond cream (p. 36) 1

4 poached pears (see p. 56) 4
or **3 cups** fresh or canned apricots **750 mL**

1 recipe apricot glaze (p. 56) *or* sifted icing sugar, for decoration 1

METHOD

Preheat oven to 375°F (190°C).

1. Prepare the tart base: Spread the almond cream inside the unbaked tart shell.
2. For a pear tart: Slice the pears in half lengthwise. Scoop out the seeds, cores and stems. Slice each half pear horizontally into thin slices. Lay the pears on top of the cream, spreading them out with a knife.
3. For an apricot tart: Arrange the apricots in circles, standing up, pushed into the cream.
4. Bake the tart until the almond cream has puffed around the fruit, and is golden and cooked through, about 30 to 40 minutes. The fruit (especially the apricots) should begin to colour. Let cool on a rack. Decorate either by brushing a thin layer of apricot glaze over the cooled tart or by sprinkling some icing sugar on the sides of the tart (or both). Serve at room temperature.

Makes one 9-inch (23 cm) tart, serving 8-10 persons

Fruit Tart ~ Jardinière

INGREDIENTS

1 Sweet shortcrust pastry tart shell, blind baked (p. 15) 1

or 1 freeform puff pastry case, fully baked (p.16) 1

1 recipe light cream (p. 33) 1

Assorted fruit, such as strawberries, kiwis, pineapple, melon, raspberries, blueberries, etc.

Apricot glaze (p. 56)

METHOD

1 Fill the cooled tart shell three-quarters full with the light cream and spread into an even layer with a small spatula or the back of a spoon.

2 Prepare the fruit by removing anything that is not edible such as seeds, skins or stems. Place the fruit decoratively on the cream, taking care not to get any cream on the top side of the fruit. Be sure to cover the entire surface of the cream with fruit so that no cream is showing when done.

3 With a soft pastry brush, apply the hot apricot glaze over the fruit to form a thin, even layer on the tart. The glaze will add flavour to the tart and keep the cream filling fresh. Refrigerate until ready to serve.

Lemon Tart

INGREDIENTS

1 Sweet shortcrust pastry tart shell, blind baked (p. 15) 1

1 recipe lemon curd (p. 37) 1

Apricot glaze (p. 56) or fruit for decoration

METHOD

Preheat oven to 400°F (200°C).

1 Pour the freshly made hot lemon filling into the cooked tart shell; spread it out evenly with a small spatula or the back of a spoon and place in oven for 10 minutes to set the filling.

2 Cool completely on a rack. Refrigerate for 4 hours before glazing.

3 With a soft pastry brush, apply the hot apricot glaze over the lemon filling to form a thin, even layer on the tart. The glaze will add flavour to the tart and keep the cream filling fresh. Alternatively, decorate the tart with fresh fruit just before serving.

Makes one 9-inch (23 cm) tart, serving 8-10 persons

This traditional North American pie can also be made with nuts. It is quite rich and sweet and therefore best served in small portions. A good accompaniment to this tart is either lightly whipped Chantilly cream or ice cream. This pie can easily be made as individual tarts.

Maple Pie and Pecan Pie

Maple Pie and Pecan Pie

INGREDIENTS

1 baked sweetcrust tart shell, any style (p. 15) **1**
1 1/2 cups pecan or walnut halves (optional) **150 g**
5 egg yolks **5**
1 egg **1**
2/3 cup maple syrup **140 mL**
1 cup brown sugar, well-packed **180 g**
1/2 cup butter **125 g**
1/2 cup heavy cream **125 mL**
1/2 teaspoon salt **3 g**
1 tablespoon vanilla **15 mL**

METHOD

Preheat oven to 325°F (160°C)

1. If using, place the nuts in an even layer in the prepared tart shell.
2. Whisk all the ingredients together in a medium-sized metal bowl. Place the bowl over a pot of simmering water (bain-marie). Stir the mixture until it thickens enough to coat the back of a spoon.
3. Strain the mixture into the cooked tart shell. Carefully place the tart in the oven.
4. Bake for about 20 minutes or until the filling is set.
5. Let cool on a rack, unmould and serve at room temperature.

Makes one 9-inch (23 cm) pie, 8-10 servings, or 6 individual 4-inch (10 cm) tarts

This delicious tart can be baked a day ahead but should only be glazed the day it is served.

Chocolate Tart

INGREDIENTS

1 Sweet shortcrust pastry tart shell, half baked (p. 15) **1**

Chocolate Filling:

3 oz semisweet chocolate **90 g**
1 1/3 cups 35% cream **330 mL**
1/2 cup milk **125 mL**
1/2 cup granulated sugar **100 g**
4 eggs **4**

METHOD

Preheat oven to 325°F (160°C).

1. Chop the chocolate into small pieces and place in a medium-sized bowl.
2. In a small saucepan, boil the cream and milk together with half the sugar.
3. In a large bowl, whisk the eggs with the remaining sugar.
4. Pour a quarter of the hot cream mixture onto the chopped chocolate and whisk until smooth and shiny. Gradually add the rest of the cream into the chocolate mixture.
5. Pour the chocolate cream onto the beaten eggs. Strain the mixture into a clean bowl and then pour it into the baked tart shell (be careful, the filling is runny).
6. Bake until the filling is set and firm, about 20 minutes.
7. Cool completely before glazing.

Makes one 9-inch (23 cm) pie, serving 8-10 persons

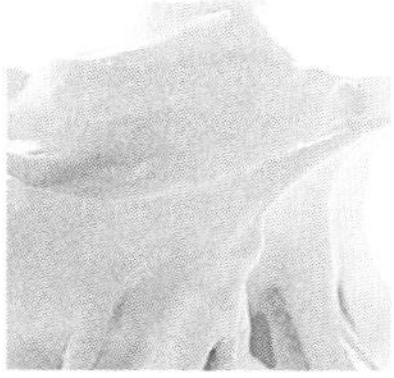

Chocolate Ganache Glaze

INGREDIENTS

6 oz bittersweet or semisweet chocolate **180 g**
1 cup 35% cream **250 mL**

METHOD

1. Chop the chocolate into small pieces with a chef's knife. Transfer the chocolate to a medium-sized bowl.
2. In a small saucepan, bring the cream to a boil. Pour half of the cream over the chocolate and stir with a wooden spoon or a rubber spatula. When the mixture is smooth, gradually stir in the remaining cream, a little at a time. Whisk the mixture until it is smooth and shiny.
3. Pour the glaze onto the centre of the cooled tart, tilting it in a clockwise motion until the glaze reaches the crust and completely coats the filling.
4. Let the glaze set at room temperature.

Serving suggestion: Serve it with a bit of Chantilly, custard cream or caramel sauce.

Classic Cakes

Classic Cakes

Technique and Tips
Mocha Cake
Simple Syrup
Black Forest Cake
Gâteau Saint-Honoré with Strawberries
Triple Chocolate Almond Cake
Chocolate Glaze
Fraisier
Vanilla Berry Charlotte
Chocolate Mousse Cake
Cheesecake
Paris-Brest
Chocolate Mascarpone Bûche de Noël

Techniques and Tips

Techniques and Tips

How to assemble and ice a cake

- Never soak a cake with warm simple syrup.
- Always level off the top of the cake if it has formed a peak when baked.
- Be careful to spread cream between layers in an even, straight layer.
- Never cut a frozen cake.
- Cakes made 24 hours in advance are easier to cut than freshly baked cakes.
- Always slice cakes with a serrated bread knife.
- Make sure to have more than enough cream to facilitate icing.
- A cake turntable greatly simplifies the task of icing cakes.
- Cakes assembled in a pastry ring can be unmoulded with the help of a blowtorch, a hot hairdryer or hot towels. Just direct the heat source to the metal ring and lift it off when the sides loosen.

- For cakes made in ring moulds, trim the layers to size using a pair of scissors.

Icing a cake

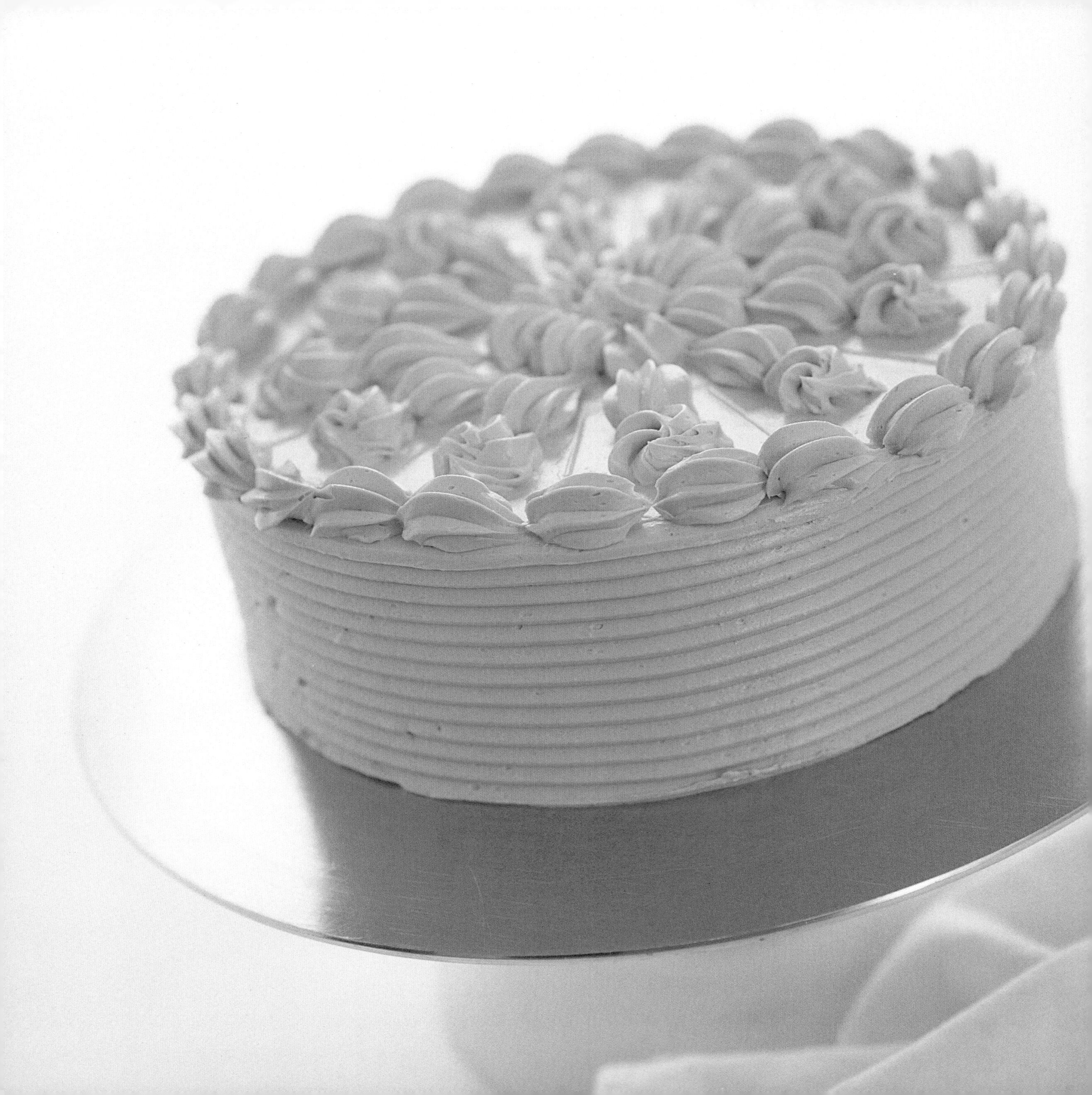

This elegant cake is delicious but must be made with care. Buttercream cakes make excellent birthday cakes.

Mocha Cake ~ Gâteau Moka

INGREDIENTS

1 cup simple syrup (recipe below) **250 mL**
1/2 cup instant coffee **125 mL**
1 recipe buttercream (p. 34) **1**
1 8-inch (20 cm) white genoise (p. 23) **1**
2 cups toasted slivered almonds for decoration (optional) **200 g**

METHOD

1. Make coffee flavouring. Bring 1/4 cup (60 mL) of simple syrup to a boil and whisk in the instant coffee. Let cool. Flavour the buttercream to taste with the coffee flavouring and pour the rest into the remaining simple syrup.
2. Cut the genoise into 3 equal slices horizontally. Set the base layer on a cardboard cut to the same size as the genoise. With a soft pastry brush, brush the base layer with about 1/4 cup (60 mL) of the coffee syrup.
3. Evenly spread a thick layer of coffee butter cream over the soaked cake. Place the second layer of cake on top of the first.
4. Repeat the process again, soaking the top layer with the remaining syrup before placing it on the cake.
5. Ice the cake with the remaining buttercream (see pictures on p. 65). If using the almonds, decorate the cake by pressing them on the sides. Pipe a decorative rosette to mark each portion.

Makes one 8-inch (20 cm) cake, serving 8-10 persons
Serving tip: Buttercream cakes should always be served at room temperature.

This syrup is used to soak and moisten cakes.
It must be refrigerated before use.

Simple Syrup ~ Sirop de base

INGREDIENTS

2 cups water **500 mL**
2 1/2 cups granulated sugar **500 g**

METHOD

1. Pour the water into a large pot and whisk in the sugar.
2. Bring to a boil over high heat, turn off the heat and let cool.
3. Strain the syrup into a clean container and keep refrigerated until needed.

This traditional German cake is a good recipe for beginners because whipped cream is easy to ice with.

Black Forest Cake

Black Forest Cake ~ FORÊT NOIRE

INGREDIENTS

1 cup top-quality bottled cherries, drained **250 mL**
1 1/2 cups simple syrup (p.67) **375 mL**
1/4 cup kirsch **60 mL**
1 8-inch (20 cm) chocolate genoise (p. 23) **1**
1 double recipe Chantilly cream (p.32) **1**
Chocolate shavings
Cherries with stems for decoration
Sifted icing sugar for decoration

METHOD

1. Twenty-four hours before assembling the cake, combine the cherries with the simple syrup and the kirsch; cover and refrigerate.
2. Strain the liquid from the cherries into a small bowl and place the cherries in another small bowl.
3. Cut the genoise into three equal slices horizontally. Set the base layer on a cardboard cut to the same size as the genoise. With a soft pastry brush, brush the base layer with about 1/4 cup (60 mL) of the reserved kirsch syrup.
4. Evenly spread a thick layer of Chantilly cream over the soaked cake
5. Spread 1/2 cup (125 mL) of cherries over the cream, spread another spoonful of cream over the cherries, and place the second layer of cake on top of the first.
6. Repeat the process again, soaking the top layer with the remaining syrup before placing it on the cake.
7. Ice the cake with the remaining cream, following the pictures on p. 65.
8. Pipe a decorative border around the cake. Put the chocolate shavings in the centre of the cake and a few fresh cherries on top to decorate.
9. Just before serving, sprinkle icing sugar over the cake.

Makes one 8-inch (20 cm) cake, serving 8-10 persons

This cake is a cross between the traditional French cake named for the patron saint of bakers, Saint-Honoré, and a strawberry tart. It is made with a puff pastry base, filled with custard and strawberries, topped with Chantilly and surrounded with caramelized, cream-filled pastry puffs called "choux", which in French means cabbage. You will need a Saint-Honoré pastry tip to help pipe the Chantilly into rounded peaks. They are available at many cake decorating stores. Any other piped Chantilly decoration is perfectly acceptable.

Gâteau Saint-Honoré with Strawberries

INGRÉDIENTS

1/2 lb puff pastry (p. 16) **225 g**
1 recipe choux pastry (p. 19) **1**
1 recipe pastry cream (p. 32) **1**
1 recipe Chantilly cream (p. 32) **1**
2 cups large strawberries, washed and stemmed **500 mL**
1 cup granulated sugar, very clean **200 g**
1/4 cup water **50 mL**

METHOD

Preheat oven to 400°F (200°C)

1 Roll out the puff pastry to a 1/4-inch (1/2 cm) thickness. Place on a parchment-lined flat baking sheet and prick the surface with a fork. Using a 9-inch (23 cm) cake pan as your guide, cut out the base circle of dough. Wrap loosely and chill.

2 Make the choux pastry. Pipe the dough around the edge of the puff pastry circle, then in a spiral starting from the centre. Pipe the remaining dough into "choux" shapes.

3 Bake the dough for 10 minutes at 400°F (200°C) then at 350°F (180°C) for another 25 minutes or until the pastry is a deep golden brown. Let cool before proceeding.

4 Whisk the pastry cream until smooth. Add a liqueur such as Kirsch to taste. Fill the baked choux with the custard using a pastry bag fitted with a small plain tip.

5 Pour the remaining custard into the centre of the baked tart and spread into an even layer.

6 Place a layer of cut berries over the surface of the custard.

7 Spread a fine layer of Chantilly cream over the berries, then with a pastry bag fitted with a star tip, cover the cream with Chantilly rosettes.

8 For the caramel: In a small pot, bring the water and sugar to a boil. When it begins to turn a caramel colour, (180°C or 350°F on a candy thermometer), remove from heat and place the base of the pot in a bowl of ice water.

9 Dip the tops of the choux in the hot caramel (be careful!).

10 Place the glazed choux around the sides of the cake. Place a large strawberry, cut side down, between each choux. Decorate the centre of the cake with a cut strawberry and serve immediately.

Makes one 8-inch (20 cm) cake, serving 6-8 persons

This cake is quite simple to make and definitely packs a chocolate punch. It is such a plain cake that good-quality chocolate is a must. It can be served with either a spoonful of Chantilly, crème anglaise or fruit coulis.

Triple Chocolate Almond Cake

INGREDIENTS

1 chocolate almond cake (p. 28) **1**

1 recipe ganache icing (p. 38) **1**

1 cup simple syrup (p. 67) **250 mL**

2 tablespoons Amaretto **30 mL**
or **1 teaspoon** almond flavouring **5 mL**

Chocolate Glaze

1/4 cup toasted slivered almonds **25 g**

METHOD

1 Cut a 9-inch (23 cm) cardboard the same size as your cake. Make sure it fits perfectly under the cake so that it is not visible from the sides.

2 Turn the cake upside down onto the cardboard. Cut the cake in half horizontally and set the top layer aside. Stir the Amaretto or almond extract into the syrup and brush some flavoured syrup onto the base of the cake.

3 Spread a thick layer of the ganache icing onto the base layer of the almond cake. Brush some flavoured syrup onto the top layer of cake and place it on top of the ganache. Ice the cake with the remaining ganache. Try to make the sides of the cake as straight as possible. The top should be flat, not rounded.

4 Place the iced cake in the freezer at least 1 hour to firm up the ganache. Prepare the glaze.

Makes one 9-inch (23 cm) cake, serving 8-10 persons

Chocolate Glaze

Since this is a glaze that must be poured on generously, this recipe is more than adequate to glaze one cake.

INGREDIENTS

4 gelatin leaves **4**

1/2 cup 35% cream **125 mL**

1/2 cup white corn syrup **125 mL**

1/3 cup water **75 mL**

1/4 cup sugar **50 g**

3/4 cup cocoa powder **60 g**

METHOD

1 Soak the gelatin leaves in plenty of cold water.

2 In a small pot, bring the cream, corn syrup, water and sugar to a boil. Whisk in the cocoa powder and return to a boil, whisking constantly. Remove from heat. Squeeze the excess water from the gelatin leaves and whisk them into the mixture.

3 Strain the hot glaze into a small bowl and keep it warm until ready to use.

4 Place the chilled cake on a wire rack with a plate or pan underneath to catch the excess glaze.

5 Pour the warm (not hot or cold) chocolate glaze directly onto the top of the prepared cake. Spread the icing with a couple of strokes of an offset spatula, being sure to ice the sides as well. Try to work as quickly as possible.

6 When the icing has set, carefully remove the cake from the metal rack, press the toasted almonds around the bottom edge of the cake and place it on a cake stand to serve.

This beautiful cake can be made in either an 8-inch spring form pan or stainless steel pastry ring.

Fraisier

INGREDIENTS

1 genoise (p. 23) 1

1 recipe mousseline cream (p. 35) 1

3 tablespoons kirsh **45 mL**

3 cups fresh strawberries, hulled **750 g**

1/2 cup simple syrup (p. 67) **125 mL**
mixed with **1 tablespoons** kirsch **15 mL**

3 1/2 oz marzipan (white almond paste) **100 g**

2 drops red food colouring 2

METHOD

1. Trim the genoise so it is flat on both sides and cut into 3 equal pieces horizontally. You will only need 2 pieces of genoise for the cake, so wrap the third piece and freeze it for future use.
2. Place the pastry ring onto a flat baking sheet lined with parchment paper. Trim the cake slices so that they both fit exactly into the mould. Place the base layer at the bottom of the mould and, with a soft pastry brush, apply a thin layer of flavoured simple syrup.
3. Spread 1/2 cup (125 mL) of the mousseline cream onto the cake base and with a small offset spatula spread it to the sides of the mould.
4. Place a row of slice or whole strawberries flush with the perimeter of the mould, then fill the centre with berries tightly placed on their sides.
5. Spread the remaining cream between the strawberries and, with a spatula, press to ensure the cream fills all the gaps.
6. Place the second cake layer over the cream, pressing down to be sure it fits snugly. Brush on a layer of simple syrup and spread on the remaining cream in a smooth layer so that the ring is filled to the top. Refrigerate until firm (overnight is best).
7. To finish, knead the marzipan with the few drops of food colouring until smooth and the colour is an even shade of bright pink. Shape the marzipan into a thin disk. Sprinkle some icing sugar on a clean surface and roll the marzipan into a 1/16-inch (3 mm) round.
8. Wrap hot towels around the cake ring and unmould the cake onto a serving plate. Immediately wash the cake ring.
9. Using the cake ring as a guide, cut a round of marzipan the same size as the top of the cake. Carefully place the cut round onto the cake. Press down lightly and decorate with a few fresh strawberries.

Serving suggestion: A red fruit coulis (p. 42) is a good accompaniment to a fraisier.

This fancy cake is a real treat in summer when fresh berries are at their ripest. For a decorative touch, tie a thick satin bow around the cake right before serving.

Vanilla Berry Charlotte

INGREDIENTS

1 recipe ladyfingers (p. 26) **1**

1/2 cup simple syrup (p. 67) **125 mL**
mixed with

1 tablespoon raspberry liqueur **15 mL**

1 recipe vanilla Bavarian cream (p. 44) **1**

1 cup fresh or frozen raspberries **250 g**

1/2 recipe Chantilly cream (p. 32) **1/2**

1 pint fresh raspberries for decoration **200 g**

Sifted icing sugar to decorate

METHOD

1 Place an 8-inch (20 cm), by 4-inch (10 cm) deep pastry ring on a parchment-lined baking sheet. Line the sides of the ring with a band of ladyfingers, sugared side out. Line the bottom of the mould with one of the genoise slices, trimming it to ensure a snug fit. With a soft pastry brush, soak the base cake layer with raspberry syrup. Trim another cake round to fit halfway up the cake and set aside.

2 The Bavarian cream should be quite thick at this point. If not, refrigerate for a few minutes.

3 Pour half the thickened cream into the prepared mould and sprinkle with half the raspberries. Place a second layer of cake and brush with more syrup. Pour on the remaining Bavarian cream and sprinkle with the remaining berries.

4 Cover the entire cake with plastic wrap and refrigerate until set, about 3 hours (the cake can be made to this point, well wrapped, and frozen for up to a month).

5 Remove the plastic wrap and pastry ring from the cake and transfer to a serving plate.

6 Spread the Chantilly cream over the top of the cake and arrange the raspberries over the cream.

7 Sprinkle the icing sugar on the berries, tie a ribbon around the cake and serve.

Makes one 8-inch (20 cm) cake, serving 10-12 persons

Serving suggestion:
A red fruit coulis (p. 42) is a good accompaniment to the charlotte.

The cake pictured is covered in chocolate curls that are beautiful but take a pastry chef's skill to master. The real importance is what is under the decoration. This cake is equally stunning when simply decorated with a dusting of rich, dark cocoa powder. You will need an 8-inch (20 cm) round, 2 1/4-inch (6 cm) high stainless steel pastry ring for this recipe.

Chocolate Mousse Cake

Chocolate Mousse Cake

INGREDIENTS

1 8-inch (20 cm) chocolate genoise (p. 23) **1**

1 recipe chocolate mousse (p. 45) **1**

1/2 cup simple syrup (p. 67) (can be flavoured with vanilla, cognac, raspberry liqueur, Grand Marnier, etc.) **125 mL**

Sifted cocoa powder for decoration

METHOD

1. Trim the cake so it is flat on both sides. Cut the genoise into 3 equal pieces horizontally.
2. Place the pastry ring onto a flat baking sheet lined with parchment paper. Trim the cake slices so that the base layer is the same size as the ring and the second one is 1 inch (2.5 cm) less in circumference. Place the base layer at the bottom of the mould and, with a soft pastry brush, apply a thin layer of flavoured simple syrup.
3. Prepare the chocolate mousse and pour one third of it over the first layer of cake. With a small spatula or the back of a spoon, spread the mousse in an even layer to the sides of the mould. To avoid holes in the finished cake, be sure the mousse is spread right on the mould. Repeat the process twice and finish by smoothing the top of the mousse with an offset spatula.
4. Freeze overnight or at least 6 hours.
5. Dust the top with cocoa powder.
6. Remove ring either by placing hot towels around the sides of the mould or by heating with a hairdryer or blowtorch.
7. Place on a decorative plate and serve sliced.

Makes one 8-inch (20 cm) cake, serving 8-10 persons
Serving suggestion: Crème anglaise is a good accompaniment to chocolate mousse cake.

Since cheesecake makes a very rich dessert, it is much better at 4 o'clock in the afternoon with coffee than after a heavy meal. This cake is thin, along the lines of a tart. For a thicker cake, just double the filling recipe. Let the cream cheese come to room temperature before starting the recipe. This will facilitate the creaming step.

Cheesecake

INGREDIENTS

Crust

3/4 cup graham cracker crumbs 100 g

Pinch salt

2 tablespoons brown sugar 25 g

3 tablespoons melted unsalted butter 45 mL

METHOD

Preheat oven to 400°F (200°C).

1 In a small bowl, combine the graham cracker crumbs, the salt and brown sugar. Add the melted butter and mix until the mixture begins to stick together. Press this mixture firmly into the bottom of an 8 or 9-inch (20 or 23 cm) springform pan. Bake in the preheated oven for 5 minutes until the crust begins to colour. Set aside.

Filling

2 cups (1 lb) cream cheese, room temperature 454 g

1/2 cup sour cream 125 mL

2/3 cup granulated sugar 150 g

2 tablespoons lemon juice 30 mL

1 teaspoon grated lemon zest 5 mL

3 eggs 3

1 teaspoon vanilla extract 5 mL

METHOD

1 In a large bowl, with an electric mixer, beat the cream cheese until it is smooth and lump free. Blend in the sour cream, half the sugar, the lemon juice and zest and beat until smooth and creamy.

2 In a small bowl, whisk the eggs with the remaining sugar and vanilla. Slowly blend the egg mixture into the cheese mixture until well combined.

3 Pour the filling over the crust in the springform pan. Bake for 5 minutes. Turn off the oven and leave the cake for 45 minutes in the closed oven until firm. The cheesecake should rise and crack.

4 If the cake is not set after 45 minutes, turn the oven on to 350°F (180°C) and bake for another 10 minutes. Let cool on a rack for 20 minutes before proceeding.

Topping

1 cup sour cream 250 mL

1/3 cup 35% cream 75 mL

3 tablespoons sugar 45 mL

1 teaspoon vanilla extract 5 mL

Fresh fruit for decoration

METHOD

Preheat oven to 350°F (180°C).

1 Whisk together the sour cream, heavy cream, sugar and vanilla. Pour onto the cooled cheesecake and spread in an even layer.

2 Bake for 10 minutes to set the topping. Let cool at room temperature. For best results, refrigerate, covered, overnight before removing the sides of the pan.

Makes one 9-inch (23 cm) cake, serving 8-10 persons
To serve: Decorate the cake with fresh fruit if desired and serve with a fruit coulis. Cut cheesecake with a sharp knife, wiping it clean after each slice.

This classic gâteau was created in the shape of a bicycle wheel by a French pastry chef to honour a bicycle race whose route ran from Paris to the city of Brest. Look for praline paste at gourmet or pastry supply stores. More praline can be added if desired.

Paris-Brest

INGREDIENTS

1 recipe choux pastry (p. 19) 1
Egg wash (p. 18)
1/4 cup blanched slivered almonds **60 g**
1 recipe mousseline cream (p. 35) 1
1/2 cup praline paste **125 g**
Icing sugar for sprinkling

METHOD

Preheat oven to 375°F (190°C). Prepare a large baking sheet with a parchment paper lining. Trace an 8-inch (20 cm) circle in pencil on the parchment paper and turn it upside down to line the baking sheet.

1. Using a pastry bag fitted with a large star tip (2/3-inch/15 mm), pipe 1 circle on the outside of the traced line, 1 circle on the inside of the traced line, and 1 circle on top of both lines. Brush with egg wash and sprinkle with the almonds.

2. Bake 20 minutes, then lower the heat to 350°F (180°C) for a further 20 minutes or until the crown of the pastry is deep golden brown and cooked through.

3. Let cool completely on a rack and either proceed with the assembly of the cake or freeze the pastry, well wrapped, for up to a month.

ASSEMBLY

1. Follow the instructions for mousseline cream, adding the praline progressively when beating the butter into the mousseline cream.

2. With a serrated bread knife, cut the choux pastry crown in half horizontally and place the base on a large plate. Using a pastry bag fitted with a star tip, pipe the cream decoratively over the base. Don't worry if it's not perfect since it will be covered. Place the top of the pastry over the cream.

3. Refrigerate at least half an hour before serving. To serve, sprinkle the surface of the cake with sifted icing sugar.

Makes one 9-inch (23 cm) cake, serving 8-10 persons

This updated version of the French Christmas classic features mascarpone mousse in a chocolate sponge cake roll, flavoured with raspberry liqueur and fresh raspberries. Fresh fruit, meringue mushrooms (p.29), pine branches or fresh holly will add a festive look to the cake.

Chocolate Mascarpone Bûche de Noël

INGREDIENTS

Mascarpone Raspberry Mousse

3/4 cup whipping cream **175 mL**

4 tablespoons raspberry liqueur **60 mL**

2 tablespoons water **30 mL**

2 1/4 teaspoons unflavoured gelatin **7 g**

6 egg yolks **6**

3/4 cup icing sugar **90 g**

1 1/2 cups mascarpone cheese, at room temperature **375 g**

1 cup fresh or frozen raspberries **250 g**

1 Chocolate Jelly Roll Cake (p. 24) **1**

1 recipe simple syrup (p. 67) with **2 tablespoons** raspberry liqueur **30 mL**

1 recipe chocolate ganache icing (p. 38) **1**

METHOD

Preparing the mousse

1. In a small bowl, whip cream until it holds firm peaks. Refrigerate.
2. Prepare a saucepan of simmering water. Pour liqueur into a large stainless steel bowl, sprinkle in the gelatin and whisk to combine. Let sit 5 minutes to soften (bloom).

3 Whisk in egg yolks and icing sugar. Place the bowl over the simmering saucepan and whisk constantly until the mixture begins to thicken, lightens in colour and doubles in volume. It should be quite warm to the touch. Remove from heat, whisk from time to time and let cool to room temperature.

4 Place the mascarpone in a small bowl and stir to soften. If it isn't at room temperature, heat over the hot water bath for a few minutes.

5 Stir a quarter of the beaten yolk mixture into the mascarpone until well blended.

6 Gradually whisk the mascarpone mixture into the remaining yolk mixture until smooth. Fold in the chilled whipped cream. The mixture should be quite thick at this point. If not, refrigerate for a few minutes.

Assembling the Cake

7 Prepare a cutting board or upside down pan the same size as the jelly roll cake and cover with a clean kitchen towel. Flip the cooled cake upside down onto the towel and carefully peel off the parchment paper. Brush with syrup. Spread mousse onto the cake and sprinkle with the fresh raspberries.

8 Roll the chilled cake toward you, using the towel to help support the cake. Place seam side down on the board, wrap in the towel and chill until set (at least 6 hours).

Finishing the Cake

9 Unwrap the cake from the towel. Slice off both ends of the cake on a diagonal. These pieces should be about 3 inches (7.5 cm) in size. Spread some icing on both sides of the cut pieces, and stick 1 piece on the top of the cake and 1 on the side to look like 2 trimmed branches. Spread the entire cake with a thick layer of icing and, with a fork or cake decorating comb, make shallow vertical ridges in the icing to resemble bark. Transfer carefully to a serving platter.

10 Decorate with meringue mushrooms, fresh fruit, holly and pine branches. Just before serving, sprinkle on a few tablespoons of icing sugar.

Makes 10 to 12 servings

Petits Fours

Petits Fours

Petits fours are very fancy French small cookies that can be either sweet or savoury.

Almond Tuiles
Cherry Sablés
Cats' Tongues
Madeleines
Cheese Straws
Anchovy Squares
Gougères

Tuiles were created to emulate the curved tiles on French rooftops. They are best when made super-thin and eaten on the day they are baked.

Almond Tuiles

INGREDIENTS

2/3 cup granulated sugar **125 g**
1 1/2 cups white slivered almonds **125 g**
3 tablespoons flour **25 g**
Pinch salt
3 egg whites **3**
2 tablespoons melted butter **30 mL**
1 teaspoon vanilla extract **5 mL**

METHOD

Preheat oven to 375°F (190°C). Prepare a baking sheet: spray with vegetable spray, line with a rubber Silpat® sheet or use one with a nonstick surface.

1 In a medium-sized bowl, combine the dry ingredients.

2 Stir in the egg whites, melted butter and vanilla until well mixed.

3 Drop the batter by teaspoonfuls onto the cookie sheets and, with the back of a wet fork, spread out the batter into a thin round layer.

4 Bake until sides are golden. Remove from oven, let stand for a few minutes. Carefully lift the cookies with a spatula and place them, right side up, on a rolling pin to cool in a curved shape.

Makes about 25 tuiles (3-inch/7.5 cm)
Storage: In a airtight box to keep them crisp.

These French cookies are the classic piped shortbreads popular at tea time and Christmas. They can be decorated with dry fruit such as apricots, figs or dates. Avoid using nuts, which tend to fall out of the baked cookies.

Cherry Sables

INGREDIENTS

1 cup unsalted butter, room temperature **200 g**
1 cup icing sugar, sifted **115 g**
1 egg **1**
1 egg yolk **1**
2 teaspoons vanilla extract **10 mL**
1 3/4 cups all-purpose flour **260 g**
Red glacé cherries for decoration

METHOD

Preheat oven to 350°F (180°C). Prepare a baking sheet: spray with vegetable spray, line with parchment paper or a rubber Silpat® sheet, or use one with a nonstick surface.

1. In a medium-sized bowl, cream the butter with the icing sugar until light and fluffy.
2. Blend in the egg and yolk, followed by the vanilla and finally the flour. Stir until combined. Do not overmix or the cookies will be tough.
3. Using a pastry bag fitted with a large star tip (2/3 inch/15 mm), pipe out cookies about 1/2 inch (1 cm) from each other in desired shapes on the baking sheets, placing a half cherry on each cookie, if desired.
4. Bake until cookies begin to colour around the edges, about 10 minutes.
5. Let cool before serving.

Makes about 70 cookies
Storage: In an airtight box to keep them crisp.

These long, thin cookies resemble little cats' tongues in shape. For an interesting variation, try piping them into much larger and longer shapes (lions' tongues). These cookies make a wonderful accompaniment to fruit salad.

Cats' Tongues ~ Langues de Chat

INGREDIENTS

1/3 cup unsalted butter, room temperature **75 g**
1 cup and 2 tablespoons icing sugar, sifted **125 g**
3 egg whites **3**
2/3 cup all-purpose flour, sifted **100 g**
1 teaspoon vanilla extract **5 mL**

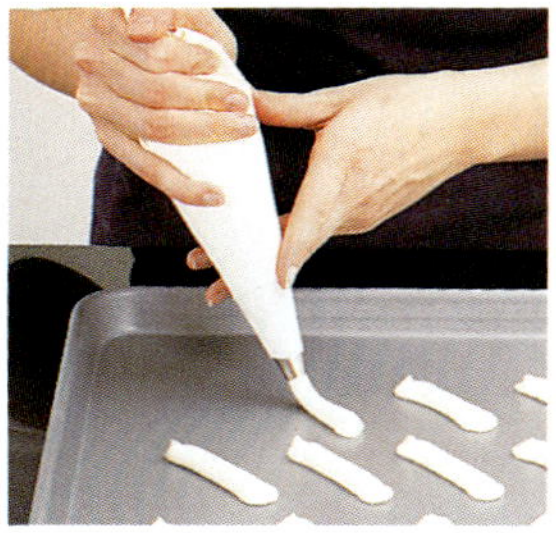

METHOD

Preheat oven to 350°F (180°C). Prepare a baking sheet: either sprayed with vegetable spray, lined with parchment paper or a rubber Silpat® sheet, or one with a nonstick surface.

1. In a medium-sized bowl with a wooden spoon, cream the butter with the icing sugar until light and fluffy.
2. Stir in the egg whites one at a time, being sure the mixture is smooth before incorporating more whites.
3. Blend in the flour and vanilla and stir until smooth.
4. With the help of a pastry bag fitted with a small round tip (1/3 inch or 1 cm), pipe out cookies about 1/2-inch from each other diagonally in bands 2 1/2 inches (6 cm) long.
5. Bake until cookies begin to colour around the sides, about 5 minutes.
6. Let cool before serving.

Makes about 50 cookies
Storage: In a airtight box to keep them crisp.

These small shell-shaped sponge cakes are often served at tea-time since they are perfect for dunking. Madeleines are best when eaten warm from the oven — before their crusty shell has the chance to soften.

Madeleines

INGREDIENTS

2 eggs **2**
1/3 cup granulated sugar **70 g**
2 tablespoons dark brown sugar **20 g**
Pinch salt
1 teaspoon vanilla **5 mL**
2/3 cup all-purpose flour, sifted **100 g**
1 teaspoon baking powder **2.5 g**
7 tablespoons butter, melted and cooled **100 g**

METHOD

1. Beat the eggs with the sugar and salt. Add the vanilla.
2. Gently fold the flour and baking powder into the mixture.
3. Gently stir in the melted butter until the mixture is smooth and shiny.
4. Cover and refrigerate about 30 minutes or until the mixture is firm.

Preheat oven to 425°F (220°C). Butter and lightly flour the madeleine mould or better yet, use a nonstick vegetable spray.

5. With the help of a pastry bag fitted with a small round tip, fill the madeleine moulds 3/4 full and bake for 5 minutes for small madeleines and 10 minutes for full-sized madeleines.
6. Let cool until they are just warm and serve immediately.

Makes 12 large or 36 small cakes

These pastries are the traditional accompaniment to the aperitif before dinner. For an even cheesier flavour, the puff pastry can be rolled in Parmesan cheese instead of flour.

Cheese Straws ~ Pailles au fromage

Ingredients

1/4 lb block of puff pastry (p. 16) **125 g**

1/2 cup Parmesan cheese (optional) **125 mL**

1 cup grated cheese (such as Gruyère, strong cheddar, or a combination of both) **250 mL**

Egg wash (p. 18)

Method

1. Sprinkle some finely grated cheese onto a clean work surface (you can use flour instead). Roll the puff pastry into a large 8- by 10-inch (20 by 25 cm) rectangle. Prick the entire surface with a fork. Lightly brush the surface with egg wash and sprinkle the grated Gruyère and/or cheddar over it.
2. Using a ruler and a sharp knife, cut the pastry lengthwise into 1-inch (2.5 cm) strips (you should get 8). Then cut it in the opposite direction into 2-inch (5 cm) pieces (you should get 5). Transfer the cut strips to a parchment-lined baking sheet and freeze.

Preheat oven to 400°F (200°C).

3. Place as many cheese straws as desired on a baking sheet and bake until golden, about 15 minutes.
4. Serve hot.

Makes 40 straws

These delicious little pastries definitely pack a punch! It is best to use refrigerated oil-packed anchovies for this recipe. For fish lovers only!

Anchovy Squares ~ Alumettes aux anchois

INGREDIENTS

1/4 lb block of puff pastry (p. 16) **125 g**
12 anchovy fillets **12**
Egg wash (p. 18)

METHOD

1 Roll the puff pastry on a floured surface into a large 8- by 10-inch (20 by 25 cm) rectangle. Lightly brush the surface with egg wash. Lay the anchovies in straight lines along half the surface of the dough (see photo). Fold the dough in half to cover the anchovies.

2 Using a ruler and a sharp knife, cut the pastry lengthwise into strips between the anchovies. Then cut it in the opposite direction into squares. Brush eggwash over each square. Transfer the pastries to a parchment-lined baking sheet and freeze.

Preheat oven to 400°F (200°C).

3 Place as many anchovy squares as desired on a baking sheet and bake until golden, about 15 minutes.

4 Serve hot.

Makes 40 squares

These sophisticated French cheese puffs should be served warm from the oven.

Gougères

INGRÉDIENTS

5 eggs **5**
1/2 cup water **125 mL**
1/2 cup milk **125 mL**
7 tablespoons unsalted butter **100 g**
1/2 teaspoon salt **3 g**
1 cup all-purpose flour **150 g**
1 cup grated gruyere cheese or sharp cheddar **250 mL**
1/4 teaspoon pepper **2 g**
Pinch nutmeg

METHOD

Preheat oven to 375°F (180°C). Prepare a baking sheet either: sprayed with vegetable spray, lined with parchment paper or a rubber Silpat® sheet, or one with a nonstick surface.

1. Crack the eggs into a large measuring cup and whisk until smooth
2. In a medium sized pot, bring the water, milk, butter and salt to a boil, stirring from time to time.
3. Remove from heat and add the flour all at once. Stir with a wooden spoon until it forms a thick pasty dough.
4. Return the pot to medium heat and stir the mixture vigorously until it begins to stick to the bottom of the pot and pull away from the sides.
5. Transfer the dough to a medium sized bowl and begin stirring in the whisked eggs, about two tablespoons at a time, only adding more egg when the mixture is homogenous.
6. Check consistency of the dough: it should shiny and smooth yet hold its shape and not be runny. Stir in 3/4 of the grated cheese, the pepper and the nutmeg.
7. Prepare a pastry bag fitted with a medium sized round tip. Fill with the dough, and pipe round ("choux") shapes onto a parchment paper.
8. Sprinkle the remaining cheese on the top.
9. Bake for about 20 minutes or until the gougères are golden brown and well-puffed.

Serve warm.

Storage: Wrap well. Freezer : 2 weeks.

Yeast Breads

Yeast Breads

Techniques and Tips
Country Bread
Olive Bread
Multigrain Bread
Braided Egg Bread
Pizza Dough
Croissants
Danish Pastry

Techniques and Tips

Techniques and Tips

Bread flour: Because of its high gluten content, bread flour is essential for these recipes. Look for it in health food stores and gourmet specialty shops. Breads made with all-purpose flour will not develop fully, resulting in a heavy loaf.

Proofing yeast and water temperature: Be especially careful with water temperature. Some yeasts call for warm water to help dissolve the granules. Water that is too hot will kill the yeast. Ideally, the water should be warm to the touch — like a baby's bath. Be sure the yeast is activated (begins to bubble) before proceeding with the recipe. Some instant yeasts can be added directly to the flour. Read the instructions on the package before starting your recipe.

Room temperature: Yeast breads can be made in a cold room but they will take much longer to rise. If the room is too warm, the dough will rise too quickly which often results in a sour-tasting bread. A good place to let dough rise is on the top of a heated oven. Be sure the dough is well-wrapped and covered with a thick towel to keep out any drafts.

Kneading: Don't hesitate to be rough with the dough when kneading. Pick it up in your hand, raise it over your head and slap it down onto a hard surface. Turn over the dough, pick it up by the side and repeat the process. Dough made by hand can take up to 10 minutes of kneading to achieve the desired consistency. You can also knead dough in a commercial mixer using a dough hook. Be careful not to overwork the dough. Cut the kneading time in half when kneading by machine. Do not make bread dough with food processors, which tend to tear the dough apart.

First, second, final rise: Yeast breads need to rise and deflate to slowly diminish the powers of the yeast. Do not judge the rising times by minutes but rather by the dough appearance. The times given are all estimates. Look at the dough instead. If after an hour it has not yet doubled in volume, let it rise a little longer. Be sure the dough is always wrapped, especially at the final rising. If not, it will form a crust and not rise properly.

The boule

The demi

Shaping bread

The boule: After the second rising, punch down the dough and cut in half if desired. Turn all the edges underneath the centre of the dough to form a round ball. Roll the ball on a clean surface, catching a bit of the dough under the base of your hand to seal the bottom of the boule. The top and sides of the boule should be very smooth.

The demi: Pound the dough into a short, fat rectangle. Roll one third of the dough towards you and push the edges down to seal the fold. Roll the second third towards you and seal the roll closed. Push down with your hands and roll the dough into a longer loaf. Roll the corners into rounded points.

Slashing the dough before baking: Breads should be slashed to allow expansion when baking. Many bakers use a razor blade, but a sharp serrated knife works well for home baking. Experiment by slashing in different patterns at different angles. Slashes should be no more than a 1/2-inch (1 cm) deep and only be made immediately before baking.

Baking to form a crust: Steam is needed in the baking process to form a crisp crust on your dough. You can place a pan in the bottom of your oven and add water right before baking to create steam. A water mister can be used to spray the inside of your oven before and just after the bread begins to bake. Be sure your oven is always preheated to the correct temperature before baking.

When is it done? Baked bread should be deep golden brown in colour. For even baking, turn the loaf halfway through the baking time. A correctly baked loaf should sound hollow when tapped on the bottom.

The best country-style breads are made with sourdough starters, resulting in a tangy flavour and crispy crust. Unfortunately this kind of bread takes at least two days to complete. This recipe can be made in one day and calls for rye flour which, though not as tasty as the sourdough, gives the bread a more rustic flavour than standard white bread.

Country Bread ~ Pain de Campagne

INGREDIENTS

2 teaspoons dry yeast **6 g**

1 1/4 cups warm water **310 mL**

1 teaspoon sugar **3 g**

2 1/2 cups bread flour **375 g**

1/2 cup rye flour **75 g**

2 teaspoons salt **15 g**

METHOD

1 Sprinkle the dry yeast over the warm water. Stir in the sugar. When the mixture begins to bubble, stir in the flour, rye flour and salt.

2 Knead the dough on a lightly floured surface for a good 10 minutes or until it's smooth and elastic.

3 Placè the ball of dough in a large oiled bowl. Cover with a clean dish towel or plastic wrap and let rise in a warm place for an hour. Punch down the dough, wrap again, and let rise until doubled in bulk (at least another hour).

Preheat oven to 450°F (230°C). Place a shallow pan in the bottom of the oven. Have a water mister on hand.

4 Turn the dough out onto a floured surface and divide it in half. Cover with a clean towel and let rise on the table for 10 minutes.

5 Roll the dough into a ball shape (boule).

6 Place the shaped loaf on a parchment-lined baking sheet, cover and let rise in a warm place until doubled in size (between 30 and 45 minutes). When the loaf is ready to be baked, it should not spring back when pressed.

7 Lightly flour the surface of the bread, and with a very sharp bread knife cut slashes 1/2-inch (1 cm) deep into the loaf in a criss-cross patern on the top of the boule.

8 Working quickly, place the loaf in the oven and pour 1 cup of warm water into the pan at the base of the oven to produce steam.

9 Close the oven door, wait 5 minutes, open the oven door and with a water mister, mist the oven for 30 seconds. Avoid the oven light (it could burst).

10 Bake the bread for about 15-20 minutes or until it is a deep golden brown.

11 Cool on a wire rack. Be sure the bread has cooled completely before slicing.

Makes 1 large round loaf

Olive Bread

METHOD

1. Proceed as for country bread (p. 100) and add 1 tablespoon (15 mL) finely chopped fresh rosemary and/or thyme and 2 tablespoons (30 mL) olive oil to the dough before kneading.
2. Knead 1/2 cup (about 12 large olives) pitted and roughly chopped black olives (Kalamata are best) into the dough before the first rise.
3. The dough can be shaped into either one large or two small boules.
4. Be sure to make a 1/2-inch (1 cm) deep slash in the dough with a serrated bread knife before baking (see country bread).

Multigrain Bread

INGREDIENTS

1 1/4 cups warm water **310 mL**

1 teaspoon dry yeast **3 g**

1 tablespoon honey **15 mL**

1 1/4 cups bread flour **340 g**

1/3 cup whole-wheat flour **50 g**

1/4 cup rye flour **50 g**

2 tablespoons bran **10 g**

2 teaspoons salt **12 g**

3/4 cup combination of sesame, flax and sunflower seeds **185 g**

1 egg, lightly beaten **1**

METHOD

1 Sprinkle the dry yeast over the warm water. Stir in the honey. When the mixture begins to bubble, stir in the remaining ingredients and all but 3 tablespoons of the seed mix.

2 Knead the dough on a lightly floured surface for a good 10 minutes or until it's smooth and elastic.

3 Place the ball of dough in a large oiled bowl. Cover with a clean dish towel or plastic wrap and let rise in a warm place for an hour. Punch down the dough, wrap again, and let rise until doubled in bulk (at least another hour).

Preheat oven to 400°F (200°C). Place a shallow pan in the bottom of the oven.

4 Turn the dough out onto a lightly floured surface and follow the instructions to form into a 12-inch (30 cm) demi loaf shape (p. 99).

5 Let the loaf rise in a warm place until doubled in size (about 45 minutes). When the loaf is ready to be baked, it should not spring back when pressed.

6 Brush the surface of the bread with the beaten egg and sprinkle on the remaining seed mix. With a very sharp serrated knife cut two 1/2-inch (1 cm) deep, long slashes into the side of the loaf from point to point on an angle.

7 Working quickly, place the loaves in the oven and pour 1 cup (250 mL) of warm water into the pan at the base of the oven to produce steam.

8 Close the oven door, wait 5 minutes, open the oven door and with a water mister, mist the oven for 30 seconds. Avoid the oven light (it could burst).

9 Bake the bread for about 20-25 minutes or until it is a deep golden brown.

10 Let the baked loaf cool on a wire rack. Be sure the bread has cooled completely before slicing.

Makes 1 large loaf

This bread is sweeter and richer than a standard the bread and is lovely toasted and spread with jam. If you find the four-strand braid too difficult, you can divide the dough into three pieces and make a three-strand braid.

Braided Egg Bread

INGREDIENTS

1 cup warm milk **250 mL**
2 teaspoons yeast **6 g**
2 tablespoons sugar **25 g**
1 1/2 teaspoons salt **9 g**
1 tablespoon honey **15 mL**
2 egg yolks **2**
1 egg **1**
2 tablespoons melted butter **30 mL**
3 cups bread flour **450 g**
Egg wash (p. 18)

METHOD

1 Sprinkle the dry yeast over the warm milk. Stir in the sugar. When the mixture begins to bubble, stir in the honey, egg yolks, egg, butter, flour and salt.

2 Knead the dough on a lightly floured surface for a good 10 minutes or until it's smooth and elastic.

3 Place the ball of dough in a large oiled bowl. Cover with a clean dish towel or plastic wrap and let rise in a warm place for an hour. Punch down the dough, wrap again, and let rise until doubled in bulk (at least another hour).

Preheat oven to 400°F (200°C).

4 Turn the dough out onto a floured surface and divide it into 4 equal pieces. Roll the four pieces into small balls. Cover with a clean towel and let rise for 10 minutes.

5 Working with one piece at a time, pound each ball flat then roll into a long rope, about 30 inches (75 cm) long. Repeat the process with all the balls. Keep each piece covered with plastic as you roll the others.

6 Working with two pieces at a time, place the pieces in a cross and braid as pictured. Repeat the process for the second braid.

7 Place both braids on a parchment-lined baking sheet, cover and let rise in a warm place until the loaves have doubled in size (between 30 and 45 minutes). When the loaves are ready to be baked, they should not spring back when pressed.

8 Brush the surface and sides of the braids with some egg wash.

9 Bake the bread for about 25 minutes or until it is a deep golden brown.

10 Cool on a wire rack. Be sure the braids have cooled completely before slicing.

Makes 2 braided loaves

This recipe makes a crisp, thick or thin crust. The toppings are up to you.

Pizza Dough

INGREDIENTS

4 teaspoons dry yeast **12 g**
1 1/2 cups warm water **375 mL**
1 teaspoon sugar **7 g**
3 1/2 cups all-purpose flour **525 g**
1/2 cup rye flour **75 g**
1/4 cup olive oil **50 mL**
2 teaspoons salt **12 g**

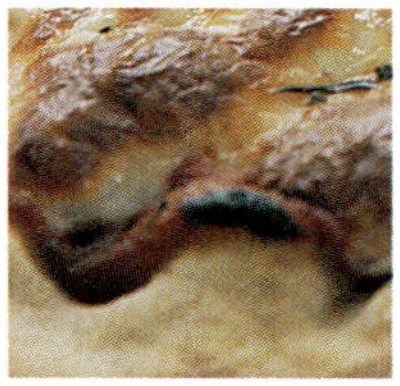

METHOD

1. In a large bowl, proof yeast in water and sugar.
2. When foamy, stir in the flour, olive oil and finally the salt. Combine well. The dough should be a bit sticky.
3. Knead the dough on a floured surface for about 7 minutes or until it's smooth and elastic.
4. Place the ball of dough in a large oiled bowl. Cover with a clean dish towel or plastic wrap and let rise in a warm place for an hour. Punch down the dough, wrap again, and let rise until doubled in bulk.
5. At this point, divide it into three sections. You can either use the dough immediately or refrigerate or freeze it for later use. It can be refrigerated for about three days, frozen for a month. Be sure the dough is kept well wrapped at all times. Frozen dough should be defrosted in the refrigerator.

To make a pizza

Preheat oven to 500°F (260°C). A pizza stone or tile is best for making pizza, but the pizza can also be made with good results in a pizza pan or on a baking sheet.

1. Working with one section of dough at a time, form the dough into a large round disk. Place it on a well-floured surface and with the tips of your fingers push over the entire surface of the dough to enlarge the surface. Continue this motion until the dough is 1/8 inch (4 mm) thick. If you aren't having much success, you can use a rolling pin.
2. Cover the pizza with desired topping and bake for 6-8 minutes or until the toppings are golden and the crust is crisp.

Makes three 9-inch (23 cm) pizza crusts

These croissants are flaky and buttery — definitely better than store-bought. They can be difficult to make at home because of the timing. Unless you plan on getting up at 4 a.m., you'll have to make them in the evening to be served, re-heated, the next morning. Once you've mastered puff pastry, croissants are a breeze since there are 4 instead of 6 turns to the dough.

Croissants

INGREDIENTS

1 cup warm milk **250 mL**

2 teaspoons dry yeast **9 g**

2 tablespoons sugar **25 g**

1 teaspoon salt **7 g**

1 cup and **3 tablespoons** bread flour **175 g**

1 cup all-purpose flour **150 g**

2/3 cup unsalted butter, room temperature **150 g**

Egg wash (p. 18)

METHOD

1. Sprinkle the dry yeast over the warm milk. Stir in the sugar. When the mixture begins to bubble, stir in the salt and flour.
2. Knead the dough on a lightly floured surface until smooth, elastic and moist (about 5 minutes).
3. Place the ball of dough in a large, lightly buttered bowl. Cover with a clean dish towel or plastic wrap and let rise in a warm place until doubled in volume (1 hour). Carefully punch down the dough to deflate it, wrap again, and refrigerate overnight.
4. On a lightly floured surface, roll the dough into a rectangle of about 15 by 9 inches or (38 by 23 cm). Spread butter on two thirds of the dough. Fold in three, being sure the unbuttered side is folded inward first (see picture).
5. Place the buttered dough on a floured baking sheet, wrap and refrigerate until the butter is firm (about 30 minutes).
6. On a lightly floured surface, roll the dough into a slightly larger rectangle and make a turn as though it were puff pastry. Repeat the process and refrigerate one hour.
7. Repeat the two turns again, always rolling the dough into a rectangle the same size. You should have four turns in all. Refrigerate again for an hour.

Preheat oven to 375°F (190°C).

8. Roll the dough again into a rectangle, but this time a bit longer about 25 by 8 inches (60 by 20 cm) and 1/8 inch (3 mm) thick.

Makes about 12 croissants

9 With a sharp knife or pizza cutter, cutting on a slant, cut the dough into 12 long triangles, every 4 inches (10 cm).

10 Make a 1-inch (2.5 cm) cut on the wide end of each triangle, stretch apart the base and roll the croissants.

11 Place the croissants on a parchment-lined or greased and floured cookie sheet, at least 2 inches (5 cm) apart. Lightly cover with plastic wrap so they don't form a crust and let rise in a warm place until doubled in volume (about 1 hour and 15 minutes).

12 Glaze with egg wash and bake until golden, about 20 minutes, being sure to turn the tray after 10 minutes for even colouring.

13 Cool on a rack.

These buttery danishes are irresistible and can be frozen and defrosted in the refrigerator as needed. You can top the danish with any jam you like. A spoonful of pastry cream (p.32) is equally delicious. This dough can also be substituted for French brioche dough.

Danish Pastry

INGREDIENTS

1/2 cup milk **125 mL**
1/4 cup sugar **50 g**
1/4 cup unsalted butter **55 g**
1 tablespoon dry yeast **5 g**
1 teaspoon salt **7 g**
2 eggs **2**
2 cups all-purpose flour **300 g**
2/3 cup unsalted butter **150 g**
Egg wash (p. 18)
1 tablespoon cinnamon **6 g**
3 tablespoons sugar **35 g**
Raspberry *or* apricot jam
1 cup simple syrup (p. 67) **250 mL**
1 tablespoon milk **15 mL**
1/2 cup icing sugar **60 g**

METHOD

1 Whisk together the milk, sugar and 1/4 cup (50 g) of butter in a small pot and heat until warm to the touch. Transfer to a bowl and sprinkle over the yeast. When the mixture begins to bubble, stir in the salt, the eggs and flour.

2 Knead the dough on a lightly floured surface until just combined — no more than 30 seconds.

3 Place the ball of dough in a large, lightly buttered bowl. Cover with a clean dish towel or plastic wrap and let rise in a warm place until doubled in volume (about 45 minutes) Carefully punch down the dough to deflate it, wrap again, and refrigerate overnight.

4 On a lightly floured surface, roll the dough into a rectangle of about 15 by 9 inches (38 by 23 cm). Spread butter on two thirds of the dough. Fold in three, being sure the unbuttered side is folded inward first (see picture).

5 Place the buttered dough on a floured baking sheet, wrap and refrigerate until the butter is firm (about 30 minutes).

6 On a lightly floured surface, roll the dough into a slightly larger rectangle and make a turn as though it were puff pastry. Repeat the process and refrigerate one hour.

7 Repeat the two turns again, always rolling the dough into a rectangle the same size. You should have four turns in all. Refrigerate again for an hour.

Preheat oven to 350°F (180°C).

8 Roll the dough again into a rectangle, but this time a bit longer and wider about 26 by 12 inches (65 by 30 cm) and 1/8 inch (3 mm) in thickness.

9 Brush the entire surface of the dough with a thin layer of egg wash. Mix together the cinnamon and sugar and sprinkle it (lengthwise) over the bottom half of the dough. Fold the dough in half, lengthwise. Roll the dough lightly to seal shut. Cut the dough into 1 1/4-inch (3 cm) bands.

10 Twist the bands in opposite directions and roll into even ropes. Cross the two ends twice and press the two ends on the opposite side of the dough to form a round danish. Turn over and place on a parchment-lined or greased and floured cookie sheet, at least 2 inches (5 cm) apart. Lightly cover with plastic wrap so the danishes don't form a crust and let rise in a warm place until doubled in volume.

11 Glaze with egg wash and spoon a bit of jam on the top.

12 Bake until golden, about 20-30 minutes.

13 Heat the simple syrup to a boil in a small pot and brush it onto the danishes immediately after they come out of the oven.

14 Let cool on a rack. Mix the milk and icing sugar together to make an icing, and with a spoon, dribble some over the top of each danish.

Makes about 14 danish pastries

Quick Breads

Quick Breads

Banana Bread
Pumpkin Pecan Tea Cake
Pound Cake
Marble Cake
Cinnamon Nut Coffee Cake
Orange Lemon "Weekend" Cake
Carrot Muffins
Blueberry Muffins

This banana bread is quite different from most recipes in that it includes the addition of olive oil. Don't be alarmed the fruity flavoured oil is an excellent enhancement to the banana flavour.

Banana Bread

INGREDIENTS

1 3/4 cups all-purpose flour **265 g**
2 teaspoons double-action baking powder **10 g**
1/4 teaspoon baking soda **1 g**
1/2 teaspoon salt **2 g**
2 eggs **2**
2/3 cup granulated sugar **125 g**
1/3 cup extra-virgin olive oil **75 mL**
1 cup mashed bananas (2 or 3) **250 mL**

METHOD

Preheat oven to 350°F (180°C). Brush the inside of a 9- by 5-inch (23 x 12.5 cm) loaf pan with melted butter and a sprinkling of flour or use a nonstick spray.

1. Sift together the flour, baking powder, baking soda and salt onto a piece of parchment paper.
2. In a large bowl with a electric mixer, beat the eggs with the sugar at high speed until doubled in volume. Blend in the olive oil.
3. Alternately stir in the sifted dry ingredients and banana purée.
4. Pour the batter into the prepared mould and place in the preheated oven.
5. Bake for 55 minutes to 1 hour. Let cool on a rack 10 minutes, unmould and let cool completely before slicing.

Makes one 9- by 5-inch (23 by 12.5 cm) loaf

This spicy cake resembles gingerbread. Half a cup of golden raisins can be added along with the pecans for an even moister cake. The frosting is optional.

Pumpkin Pecan Tea Cake

INGREDIENTS

3/4 cup pecan halves **75 g**
1 1/2 cups all-purpose flour **225 g**
1 teaspoon salt **6 g**
1 teaspoon baking soda **5 g**
1 teaspoon baking powder **5 g**
1 teaspoon cinnamon **4 g**
1 teaspoon ground ginger **4 g**
1/4 teaspoon ground cloves **1 g**
1/4 teaspoon mace **1 g**
1 stick of unsalted butter of 3.5 oz (100 g) **1**
1 cup brown sugar, firmly packed **200 g**
2 eggs **2**
1 cup pumpkin purée **250 mL**

METHOD

Preheat oven to 350°F (180°C). Butter and flour a 9-inch (23 cm) loaf pan.

1 Toast the pecans in the preheated oven for 7 minutes. Let cool and chop them into rough pieces.

2 Sift together the flour, salt, baking powder, baking soda and spices.

3 In a large bowl, with an electric mixer, cream the butter with the brown sugar until light and fluffy. Beat in the eggs one at a time. Alternatly stir in the dry ingredients and the pumpkin purée. Gently fold in the pecans. Do not overmix the batter or the bread will be tough.

4 Spoon the mixture into the prepared mould. Bake for 30 minutes for small cakes or muffins, and for 50 minutes for a large loaf. Let cool completely before frosting.

Frosting

INGREDIENTS

1 stick unsalted butter of 3.5 oz (100 g) **1**
1 package cream cheese of 4 oz (125 g) **1**
1/2 teaspoon maple essence *or* vanilla extract **2 mL**
1 cup icing sugar, sifted **115 g**
1/4 cup pecans, roughly chopped **30 g**

METHOD

1 In a medium-sized bowl, with an electric mixer, beat the butter and cream cheese together until very light and fluffy. Add the maple essence or vanilla extract and beat in the icing sugar until the frosting is smooth.

2 Ice the top of the cake when it has cooled completely and sprinkle on the chopped pecans.

Makes one, 9- by 5-inch (23 x 12.5 cm) loaf

This pound cake recipe is unusual in that it includes beaten egg whites, resulting in a lighter cake with a crispy crust.

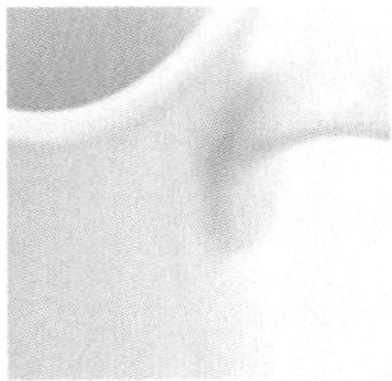

Pound Cake

INGREDIENTS

- **6** egg yolks **6**
- **1 cup** granulated sugar **200 g**
- **1 cup** butter, melted and cooled **225 g**
- **2 teaspoons** vanilla extract **10 mL**
- **2 cups** pastry flour, sifted **250 g**
- **1 teaspoon** baking powder **5 g**
- **6** egg whites **6**
- **1/2 cup** granulated sugar **100 g**

METHOD

Preheat oven to 350°F (180°C). Butter and flour a 9-inch (23 cm) loaf pan.

1. In a large bowl with an electric mixer, beat the egg yolks at high speed, gradually adding the sugar. Continue beating until the mixture has doubled in volume and is pale in colour.
2. Beat in the melted butter and vanilla extract.
3. With a rubber spatula, fold in the sifted flour and baking powder.
4. In a medium-sized clean bowl, using an electric mixer, beat the egg whites at high speed, gradually adding the sugar, until they form firm peaks.
5. Fold the beaten whites into the base mixture and pour the batter into the prepared mould.
6. Place in the preheated oven and bake for 30-40 minutes or until a cake tester comes out clean.
7. Let cool on a rack. Unmould and let cool completely before slicing.

Marble Cake (variation)

METHOD

Preheat oven to 350°F (180°C). Butter and flour a 9-inch (23 cm) loaf pan.

1. Prepare the pound cake mixture.
2. In a small bowl, whisk 1/4 cup (20 g) of cocoa with 3 tablespoons (45 mL) of milk. Place one third of the batter in a small bowl and whisk in the diluted cocoa.
3. Spoon half the vanilla batter in the bottom of the mould, followed by the chocolate layer, and top it off with the other half of the vanilla mixture.
4. Run a spoon in spirals around the batter.
5. Bake for 30-40 minutes or until a cake tester comes out clean.
6. Let cool on a rack. Unmould and let cool completely before slicing.

Makes one, 9- by 5-inch (23 by 12.5 cm) loaf

Coffee cake can be served at any time of day. With a scoop of ice cream it would even make an excellent dessert. This large cake is enough to serve a crowd.

Cinnamon Nut Coffee Cake

INGREDIENTS

Topping

1 cup fresh walnuts, chopped **100 g**
1/4 cup sugar **50 g**
1 tablespoon flour **10 g**
1 teaspoon cinnamon **5 g**
Pinch nutmeg
Pinch salt

Cake Mix

3 3/4 cups all-purpose flour **560 g**
3 teaspoons baking powder **15 g**
1 1/2 teaspoons baking soda **8 g**
1 1/2 teaspoons salt **8 g**
1 1/2 cups butter **330 g**
1 1/2 cups sugar **200 g**
4 eggs **4**
1 egg yolk **1**
1 tablespoon vanilla extract **15 mL**
1 1/2 cups sour cream **375 mL**

METHOD

TOPPING

1 Combine all the ingredients in a small bowl.

CAKE MIX

Preheat oven to 350°F (180°C). Generously butter a 9-inch (23 cm) angel food cake pan.

1 Sift the dry ingredients together on a piece of parchment paper.

2 With an electric mixer on high speed, cream the butter with the sugar until light and fluffy. Add the eggs and yolk one by one, mixing well after each addition. Stir in the vanilla.

3 Alternately stir in the sifted dry ingredients and the sour cream. Stir until the mixture is well combined. If the batter is over-mixed, the cake will be tough.

4 Spoon half the mixture into the cake pan. Sprinkle in half the nut topping. Spoon the remaining batter into the pan and sprinkle the remaining topping over the top.

5 Bake in the preheated oven until a cake tester comes out clean. Let cool on a rack and unmould the cake when it has cooled. Slice and serve.

Makes one 9-inch (23 cm) coffee cake of at least 12 servings

This is the easiest cake we've ever made and the results are delicious. This tea cake is called a "weekend" because it is guaranteed to stay fresh over the weekend. In fact, it is best eaten the day after it is made.

Orange Lemon "Weekend" Cake

Orange Lemon "Weekend" Cake

INGREDIENTS

1 cup and 2 tablespoons unsalted butter **210 g**
1 1/4 cups all-purpose flour **190 g**
5 eggs **5**
3/4 cup and 3 tablespoons granulated sugar **185 g**
finely grated zest of one orange

METHOD

Preheat oven to 350°F (180°C). Melt the butter on low heat until quite hot. Brush the inside of a 9- by 5-inch (23 by 12.5 cm) loaf pan with 1 tablespoon of the melted butter and 1 tablespoon of the measured flour.

1. In a medium-sized bowl, whisk the eggs with the sugar until well combined.
2. With a wooden spoon, stir in the flour until smooth. Add the remaining hot melted butter, a bit at a time, stirring after each addition, until well blended. Stir in the zest.
3. Pour the batter into the greased and floured mould, and place in the preheated oven. Bake for 45 minutes or until a wooden skewer comes out clean.
4. Unmould onto a wire rack and with a pastry brush, brush half the glaze generously over the top and sides of the cake. Let cool 15 minutes, then repeat the process with the remaining glaze.
5. Let cool completely, before slicing.

Glaze

INGREDIENTS

3 tablespoons freshly squeezed lemon juice **45 mL**
1 1/2 cups sifted icing sugar **175 g**

METHOD

1. In a small bowl, combine the ingredients and whisk until smooth. The glaze must be quite thick. Keep covered until ready to use.

Makes one 9- by 5-inch (23 by 12.5 cm) loaf

Both the carrot and blueberry muffin mixes can be made up to two days in advance and kept refrigerated until ready to bake. Nuts, raisins or chopped fruit can be added to the carrot muffins.

Carrot Muffins

Carrot Muffins

INGREDIENTS

1 2/3 cups flour **250 g**

1/2 teaspoon baking powder **3 g**

1/2 teaspoon baking soda **3 g**

1/2 teaspoon cinnamon **3 g**

1/2 teaspoon nutmeg **3 g**

1/2 teaspoon salt **3 g**

3 eggs **3**

1 cup brown sugar **235 g**

2/3 cup vegetable oil **150 mL**

1/2 teaspoon vanilla extract **2 mL**

2 cups finely grated carrot, about 6 medium carrots, peeled **275 g**

METHOD

Preheat oven to 350°F (180°C). Line a muffin pan with twelve paper muffin cups.

1. Sift the dry ingredients together on a piece of parchment paper.
2. With an electric mixer on high speed, beat the eggs with the sugar until frothy. Blend in the oil and the vanilla and beat until smooth.
3. On low speed, stir in the sifted dry ingredients and the shredded carrots. Stir until the mixture is well combined.
4. Generously fill the muffin cups with the batter.
5. Bake in the preheated oven for 30 minutes or until a cake tester comes out clean. Let cool on a rack and unmould the muffins when cool.

Makes 12 large muffins

Be careful not to over-mix the batter when incorporating the blueberries, or the muffins will turn blue.

Blueberry Muffins

INGREDIENTS

2 1/3 cups flour **350 g**
1 teaspoon salt **6 g**
2 1/2 teaspoons baking powder **13 g**
1 cup granulated sugar **200 g**
1/2 cup unsalted butter **110 g**
1 teaspoon vanilla extract **5 mL**
3 eggs **3**
1 egg yolk **1**
3/4 cup and 2 tablespoons milk **200 mL**
1 1/2 cups fresh or frozen blueberries **175 g**

METHOD

Preheat oven to 350°F (180°C). Line a muffin pan with twelve paper muffin cups.

1. Sift the dry ingredients together on a piece of parchment paper.
2. With an electric mixer on high speed, cream the butter with the sugar until light and fluffy. Add the eggs and yolk one by one, mixing well after each addition. Stir in the vanilla.
3. On low speed, stir in the sifted dry ingredients alternatly with the milk. Stir until the mixture is well combined. Fold in the blueberries.
4. Generously fill the muffin cups with the batter.
5. Bake in the preheated oven for 30 minutes or until a cake tester comes out clean. Let cool on a rack and unmould the muffins when cool.

Makes 12 large muffins

Index

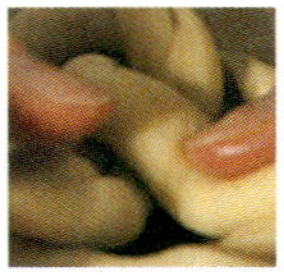

almond
- chocolate cake 28, 72
- cream 36
- pear or apricot tart 57
- tuiles 88

anchovy squares 93
apple
- pie 50
- sauce 41
- tart 53

apricot
- almond tart 57
- glaze 56

banana bread 114
bavarian 44
berry charlotte 77
Black Forest cake 69
blueberry muffins 124
braided egg bread 105
bread
- banana 114
- country 100
- egg, braided 105
- multigrain 103
- olive 101

bûche de Noël 84
buttercream 34

cake
- Black Forest 69
- chocolate almond 28
- chocolate jelly roll 24
- chocolate mousse 79
- cinnamon nut coffee 119
- marble 116
- moka 67
- pound 116
- pumpkin pecan tea 115
- orange lemon “weekend” 121
- sponge 25
- triple chocolate almond 72

caramel sauce 40
carrot muffins 123
cats’ tongues 90
Chantilly cream 32
charlotte
- vanilla berry 77

cheese straws 92
cheesecake 80
cherry sables 89
chocolate
- almond cake 28, 72
- ganache glaze 61
- glaze 72
- jelly roll cake 24
- mascarpone bûche de Noël 84
- mousse 45
- mousse cake 79
- sauce 41
- tart 61

cinnamon nut coffee cake 119
classic ganache 38
coulis,fruit 42
country bread 100
cream
- almond 36
- Chantilly 32
- custard 39
- light 33
- mousseline 35
- pastry 32

croissants 108
custard cream 39
Danish pastry 110

egg bread, braided 105
egg wash 18

fraisier 75
French apple tart 53
French meringue 29
frosting 115
fruit coulis 42
fruit mousse 43
fruit tart 58

ganache
- classic 38
- glaze 61
- icing 38

gâteau Saint-Honoré with strawberries 71
genoise 23
glaze
- apricot 56
- chocolate 72
- chocolate ganache 61

gougères 94

jelly
- chocolate roll cake 24

ladyfingers
lemon
- curd 37
- orange “weekend” cake 121
- tart 58

light cream 33

madeleines 91
maple pie 59
marble cake 116
mascarpone
- chocolate bûche de Noël 84

meringue 29
meringue mushrooms 29
moka cake 67
mousse
- chocolate 45
- chocolate, cake 79
- fruit 43

mousseline cream 35
muffins
- blueberry 124
- carrot 123

multigrain bread 103

nut
- cinnamon coffee cake 119

olive bread 101
orange lemon "weekend" cake 121

Paris-Brest 83
pastry
- choux 19
- cream 32
- danish 110
- puff 16
- shortcrust 14
- sweet shortcrust 15

pear or apricot almond tart 57
pears, poached 56
pecan
- pie 59
- pumpkin tea cake 115

pie
- apple 50
- maple 59
- pecan 59

pizza dough 107
poached pears 56
pound cake 116
pumpkin pecan tea cake 115

Saint-Honoré with strawberries 71
sauce
- apple 41
- caramel 40
- chocolate 41

simple fruit mousse 43
sponge cake 25
strawberries, gâteau Saint-Honoré 71

tart
- apple 53
- chocolate 61
- fruit 58
- lemon 58
- pear or apricot almond 57

tarte Tatin 55
techniques and Tips
- basic cakes 22
- classic cakes 63
- pies and tarts 48
- yeast breads 97

triple chocolate almond cake 72

vanilla bavarian 44
vanilla berry charlotte 77